Palgrave Advances in Work and Organizational Psychology

Palgrave Advances in Work and Organizational Psychology publishes focused, peer-reviewed books on emerging questions in the psychology of work, workers and organizations. Designed for the Palgrave Pivot format, the series provides a rapid publishing route for books examining how changing forms of work are reshaping behaviour, wellbeing, identity, motivation, performance, collaboration, leadership, careers and organizational life — and how work and organizational psychology can respond.

The series is especially suited to timely, agenda-setting work on rapidly developing areas of work and organizational psychology. These include new technologies and work arrangements, such as algorithmic management, artificial intelligence, automation and robotics at work, human-AI collaboration, hybrid and remote work, platform and gig work, and digital surveillance. They also include urgent questions around psychosocial risk, wellbeing, burnout, resilience, emotional labour, leadership and organizational change, workplace diversity, inclusion and inequality, neurodiversity and disability at work, ageing workforces, sustainable working lives, evidence-based practice and methodological innovation.

Books may advance theory, synthesize evidence, present new empirical findings, develop methods, evaluate interventions, translate research for practice or policy, or open new debates about the future of work. The series welcomes contributions from across work and organizational psychology, I-O psychology, occupational psychology, occupational health psychology and closely related fields where the psychological contribution is clear.

Palgrave Pivots are typically 25,000–50,000 words and may be single-authored, multi-authored or, where appropriate, tightly edited. Proposals should make clear why the topic needs a short book now: what debate is moving, what evidence is emerging, what theory needs rethinking, or what practical, organizational or policy problem requires a timely scholarly response.

Atte Oksanen • Iina Savolainen

AI Disruption at Work

Employee Identity, Emotion, and Adaptation

palgrave
macmillan

Atte Oksanen
Faculty of Social Sciences
Tampere University
Tampere, Finland

Iina Savolainen
Faculty of Social Sciences
Tampere University
Tampere, Finland

ISSN 3120-6557 ISSN 3120-6565 (electronic)
Palgrave Advances in Work and Organizational Psychology
ISBN 978-3-032-35206-4 ISBN 978-3-032-35207-1 (eBook)
https://doi.org/10.1007/978-3-032-35207-1

This work was supported by Tampere University.

This Palgrave Macmillan imprint is published by the registered company Springer Nature Switzerland AG.
The registered company address is: Gewerbestrasse 11, 6330 Cham, Switzerland

Praise for *AI Disruption at Work*

"*AI Disruption at Work* by Prof. Dr. Atte Oksanen and Dr. Iina Savolainen, renowned researchers on digital work and AI, is a must-read for psychologists, HR professionals, and leaders shaping the future of work. This insightful book explores how AI is transforming not just the way we work, but how we experience work itself, from identity and self-efficacy to stress and job engagement. By bridging theory with practical applications, the authors make a powerful case for human-centered, ethical AI integration, ensuring that technology enhances rather than erodes workers' autonomy, meaning, and well-being. A visionary and actionable guide—highly recommended!"

—Jessica de Bloom, Professor, *Faculty of Economics and Business, University of Groningen, The Netherlands*

"In these times of change, this book provides an extremely timely synthesis of years of experience of Prof. Dr. Atte Oksanen and Dr. Iina Savolainen, who have been substantially ahead of the curve on the path of understanding the role of AI in the workplace. This work builds on a robust empirical basis to provide an advanced social psychological perspective away from the vast majority of recent quick and light literature on this topic. I recommend this book as a solid resource to understand what we already know about AI at work and as an inspiration to what lies ahead."

—David Garcia, *Professor for Social and Behavioral Data Science, Center for Data and Methods, University of Konstanz, Germany*

"AI disruption is no longer a forecast—it is an active reality redefining roles from medicine to the arts. Through a human-centered lens and rare data spanning six continents, this book moves beyond hype to reveal how workers experience this shift emotionally and cognitively. Its landmark contribution is a social–psychological framework addressing identity threat and AI self-efficacy, providing the tools to reclaim agency in an automated world. I recommend this guide for its empirical depth and visionary roadmap toward ethical, sustainable careers. It is essential reading for leaders and scholars seeking an evidence-based strategy to ensure technology elevates, rather than erases, the human worker. In the race to build smarter machines, we must not lose the humans who work alongside them."

—Hye-Jin Paek, Professor, *Department of Advertising & Public Relations, Director, Academic Information Center and Library, Hanyang University-ERICA, South Korea*

Acknowledgments We wish to thank the Finnish Work Environment Fund, which supported the *AI Disruption at Work* Research Project 2024–2026 (project number 230330). We also extend our thanks to the organizations involved in collecting qualitative data for the project. Additionally, we thank the Finnish Cultural Foundation and Wihuri Foundation, which have supported the other data sets utilized in this work. Finally, we wish to thank the Emerging Technologies Lab researchers and the work community, as well as our collaborators.

Competing Interests The authors have no competing interests to declare that are relevant to the content of this manuscript.

Contents

About the authors

Atte Oksanen is professor of social psychology and vice dean for research at the Faculty of Social Sciences of Tampere University, Finland. Oksanen's research focuses on digital technologies, social interaction, crime, and addiction. He is the director of the Emerging Technologies Lab research center. Oksanen has successfully led several major research projects funded by the Academy of Finland, Kone Foundation, Finnish Cultural Foundation, Aaltonen Foundation, Finnish Foundation for Alcohol Studies, Finnish Work Environment Fund, Wihuri Foundation, and Helsingin Sanomat Foundation. His international research projects have been funded by the European Union, Scandinavian Research Council for Criminology, the Research Council of Norway, and the National Science Foundation (U.S.). He has published extensively on topics of social media, online communities, and cyberhate and has over 400 publications to his name, with over 220 peer-reviewed international journal articles, including flagship journals (e.g., *Criminology, Addiction, Pediatrics, International Journal of Information Management, Social Science & Medicine, Computers in Human Behavior, New Media & Society, and Higher Education*). Publications include a seminal monograph on cyberhate and cybervictimization (*Online Hate and Harmful Content: Cross-National Perspectives*, Routledge, 2017).

Iina Savolainen is a senior research fellow in the Faculty of Social Sciences at Tampere University and vice director of the Emerging Technologies Lab research center. She has a background in psychology and holds an MSc in psychological science from Tulane University in the United States, where she has lived for over 10 years. As a dual citizen of the United States and Finland, she has international academic training and research experience. Her work adopts a social psychological and interdisciplinary perspective to explore how technology and the evolving digital landscape shape human interactions and health behaviors. Savolainen has nearly 10 years of research experience in social psychology, with a particular focus on work–life themes. Her recent studies have examined remote work, COVID-19-related anxiety among workers and well-being at work in Finland. She has also investigated alcohol use and social media behavior during pandemic restrictions as well as digital stressors in the workplace. Currently, her research focuses on AI disruption at work as one of the core team members of the *AI Disruption at Work* research project. She has over 100 publications, including over 70 peer-reviewed research articles in leading journals such as *Computers in Human Behavior*, *Journal of Medical Internet Research*, *New Media & Society*, and *Communications Psychology*. Savolainen also teaches research methods at the Faculty of Social Sciences at Tampere University, one of her special teaching areas being multivariate research methods for work–life studies.

List of Abbreviations

AI	Artificial intelligence
AGI	Artificial general intelligence
AILRSE-5	5-item AI Learning Readiness Self-Efficacy Scale
EU	European Union
GenAI	Generative AI
GPU	Graphics processing unit
HR	Human resources
IT	Information technology
JD-R	Job demands-resources model
LLM	Large language model
N, n	Sample size
SDT	Self-determination theory
SelfTech-EU-6	*Self and Technology EU Six-country Longitudinal Survey*
SelfTech-GE-6	*Self and Technology Global Extended Six-country Survey*
SME	Small to medium-sized enterprise
T1 / T2 / T3	Survey time points in longitudinal datasets
WorkAI	*AI at Work Longitudinal Survey*
WorkSome	*Social Media at Work Longitudinal Survey*

List of Figures

List of Tables

CHAPTER 1

Introduction: Rewiring the Workplace

Abstract Workers around the world are confronting a transformative force: artificial intelligence (AI). Although AI has a long history, it is now reaching a level of sophistication at which its impacts can be widely felt and experienced. AI tools today are more flexible than prior technologies and thus have the capacity to transform working life in novel ways. This book offers a timely, empirical insight into AI-driven disruption at work. It traces the history of technological development leading to today's tools and focuses on the experiences of workers living and working through this transformation. Drawing on cross-national and longitudinal evidence, we offer novel perspectives on not only how AI is being used and by whom, but also how it is used and which psychosocial processes are involved in AI acceptance and use. We provide new insight into workers' coping and stress and offer a vision of the future worker.

Keywords Artificial intelligence • Work • Digital transformation

In late 2025, journalists at *The Wall Street Journal* gave control of an office vending machine to autonomous artificial intelligence (AI) agents (Stern, 2025). An AI agent called Claudius got things spectacularly wrong: it priced items to zero, ordered luxury goods, and even a live fish. It is fair

A. Oksanen, I. Savolainen, *AI Disruption at Work*, Palgrave Advances in Work and Organizational Psychology,
https://doi.org/10.1007/978-3-032-35207-1_1

to say that Claudius was not able to keep up with the challenge it was given and was not equipped to handle unpredictable interactions with the skilled journalists who, for example, tried to convince Claudius that it is a communist vending machine. The conclusion of this AI crash test was that AI's integration into the workplace still requires alignment with context. Machines are not necessarily replacing humans, but the fact that we can even talk about this type of test speaks for itself about how science fiction is becoming reality.

Working life is undergoing a visible transformation, with many jobs disappearing or changing in real time. One senior member of a software development company based in Helsinki, Finland, expressed to us that it is emotional to see things moving forward so quickly. He told a story about colleagues becoming sad because they had lost the world of coding. For a long time, coding, like writing for authors, was only what humans did, with refined skills and unique styles attached to it. Now, AI has taken over coding, and human tasks have shifted more toward refining the process. This is also reflected in the job market of the information technology sector. While there is still a need for senior staff, the number of available entry-level positions has declined.

We are based in Finland, but Iina Savolainen, the second author of this book, brings an additional perspective from having lived in the United States for over a decade. Both the United States and Finland are known as advanced digital economies with strong digital infrastructure, early and rapid adoption of technologies, and a general cultural orientation toward innovation and technology. Despite being a small Nordic country, Finland has for decades been at the forefront of technological developments and an early adopter of new technologies. In Finland, technologies are often adopted at a rapid pace before even thinking about the consequences of their use. The United States has held technological dominance over the last few decades, ensured by continuous funding and promotion of its technology sector as markets grow (Zúñiga et al., 2024). Together, these countries represent different geopolitical contexts, Finland being more centralized in EU regulation and the United States first giving lead to companies after which policy typically follows. However, they are alike in digital penetration, technologically skilled educated workforce, and strong research-focused innovation.

Changes brought about by AI development in the 2020s not only involve examples from the IT sector and coding. Similar processes regarding role changes and how the work is conducted are happening in journalism, medicine, academia, and even in the world of art. This is not simply anecdotal evidence. Despite the hype over AI, it is now evident that the current transformation is not merely about adding one more technology to workplaces. It is more comprehensive, and we cannot dismiss it by stating that we have seen it before. Even though an AI-run vending machine might not be able to successfully carry out a specific task, as demonstrated in *The Wall Street Journal* article, AI systems are already replacing the human workforce. If you are a graphic designer, translator, or working in any type of creative or knowledge-based industry, AI has most likely already infiltrated or taken part in your work.

Our book is based on recent intensive research projects at the Emerging Technologies Lab at Tampere University, Finland. We have studied intelligent technologies from a human-centered perspective for years, using a longitudinal design and covering recent developments in Finland and Europe. We also work with global data, including data from the Americas, Europe, Asia, Oceania, and Africa. Our research projects cover both the societal and human sides of new technologies. We consider the current AI transformation to be at least equivalent to the rise of social media, significantly impacting social relationships and societies throughout the world. The only difference is that this disruption might be even deeper or more profound in nature. Our focus is on people, as their role in this story is central. We will comprehensively consider their experiences and how they feel about this change.

The Age of AI

The 2020s have been defined by rapid advances in artificial intelligence and intelligent digital technologies. The background to this change is years of research and development in machine learning, especially transformer architectures in deep learning. These were combined with the large-scale datasets used in the training of the existing AI models. Developments in hardware, for example, graphics processing units (GPUs) and cloud-based infrastructures, enabled the change. Although the most visible form of development has been large language models (LLMs) and generative AI (GenAI) tools, AI solutions are beginning to be integrated into the entire digital infrastructure and everyday technological solutions. More recently, these developments have also enabled the emergence of AI agents, in other words, AI systems capable of autonomously performing sequences of tasks, interacting with digital environments, and coordinating multiple tools to accomplish complex objectives.

AI technologies generally refer to systems capable of performing tasks that typically require human intelligence and that can learn and adapt to user needs and requirements (Russell & Norvig, 2021). Developments in AI agents and agentic AI illustrate a transition from systems that primarily generate outputs to systems capable of executing tasks and coordinating increasingly complex workflows (Sapkota et al., 2025). Ultimately, AI development aims to create intelligent tools that augment human abilities. Their implementation and adoption may drive innovation, improve efficiency, and provide solutions to existing societal challenges, such as predicting climate change trends, improving diagnostics in health care, and streamlining processes across different business sectors.

AI is embedded in various systems, ranging in both function and sophistication. This widespread applicability and use present two challenges. First, as a society, we are reaching a point of usage where there is no clear return to the pre-AI era. Workers must adapt to these changes and deal with the implications AI technologies bring in terms of their work and well-being. Second, AI users differ significantly in their awareness and readiness to adapt. There are users of AI who, given its sometimes unseen nature, do not know they are, in fact, using AI, creating a discrepancy between users and their capacity to adapt. AI users form a diverse group, ranging from technology-savvy users to beginners and even oblivious users. Recent research suggests that those who have higher technological competence tend to be more cautious and critical of AI usage, whereas beginner users with lower AI literacy are more likely to adopt AI uncritically, as they often perceive it as magical and experience feelings of awe when using it (Tully et al., 2025).

This divergence among users reflects the largely unregulated and uncontrolled implementation of AI. At present, companies and institutions are largely free to develop and deploy algorithms that prioritize engagement, profit, and impact, often without sufficient consideration of how users understand, experience, or are affected by the use of AI. Before the current scope of AI applications and their widespread implementation, AI was not mainstream and had a limited impact on workers across sectors. Rather, earlier forms of AI were mostly rule based, relying on explicitly programmed logical rules and primarily focused on expert users. In contrast, today's age of AI is unique, bringing both unforeseen opportunities and challenges for companies, users, and workers.

In several professions, AI has been integrated in ways that enhance efficiency while maintaining or even improving job quality. These positive changes have been visible, especially in the human resources and management-related sectors. Notable transformation has been observed in professional and administrative roles, including consulting, accounting, finance, hospitality, marketing, and recruitment. Studies examining these occupational groups report mainly beneficial outcomes from AI implementation, especially in terms of improved processes, increased efficiency, and saving time (Horodyski, 2023; Kambur & Akar, 2022; López Jiménez & Ouariachi, 2021; Wang et al., 2023). In some fields, AI is particularly welcomed due to its potential to enhance fairness and objectivity (Kambur & Akar, 2022). As such, AI can help address prior dissatisfaction with traditional practices within these specific domains.

Despite widely positive perspectives on AI, public and academic debate about AI-driven changes to work often takes a pessimistic tone, reflecting its associations with job replacement, skill obsolescence, and extensive role restructuring (Bankins et al., 2024). However, negatively perceived consequences have often been sector-specific or unevenly distributed across occupations. Historically, more pronounced effects have been experienced in production and manufacturing sectors where automatic processes are more likely to displace labor (Acemoglu & Restrepo, 2018). More recently, AI has been applied to automate and reorganize tasks of knowledge workers (Savolainen et al., 2026). Despite their clear benefits, these developments may also contribute to fear-based worker responses, including increased perception of job insecurity, resistance to technological change and reduced organizational commitment (Bankins et al., 2024; Savolainen et al., 2026).

Our Approach and Methodology

In this book, we acknowledge the large-scale impact of AI and its societal and global significance while focusing on the human side of workers' experiences and outcomes. We review the most recent evidence on how workers have navigated the changes AI has brought to their workplaces and tasks, and what steps, if any, they have taken to adapt and adjust. Analyses of our large-scale data provide new insights into the attitudes and expectations workers hold regarding AI and its use at work. We also examine workers' prior knowledge and preparedness in the context of ongoing technological change and introduce key concepts central to this book, including identity threat, augmented self, and AI learning readiness self-efficacy.

Methodologically, our work is grounded in research that we have conducted in multiple projects at the Emerging Technologies Lab over the past few years. Our unique strength is that we started the work well before the current AI hype, and we have been able to follow the same individuals for several years across these projects. We utilize a survey research design that is highly appropriate for covering end-users' experiences of something new and unexpected. Our data sets aim to always cover the national scale, and we strive for our samples to be as representative as possible. These data sets are unique in their focus and novelty. They provide us with necessary empirical insights covering the human perspective, relying on social and occupational psychology.

The core of the findings covered consists of the work conducted in the *AI Disruption at Work* project that was funded by the Finnish Work Environment Fund during 2024–2026. The project collected an *AI at Work Longitudinal Survey* (*WorkAI*) of Finnish employees aged 18–65 who were residing in mainland Finland. Data collection was administered by the data provider company Norstat. Data were collected biannually starting in August 2024 (time point 1, T1, $N = 2117$) with follow-up survey invitations sent to all T1 respondents in T2 (spring 2025) and T3 (autumn 2025). Response rates to T2 (80 %, $n = 1680$) and T3 (70 %, $n = 1479$) were reasonably high. The sample matches the Finnish working population in terms of socio-demographic background variables and geographic area. We found no major deviances due to attrition between time points.

Additionally, the *AI Disruption at Work* project recruited interviewees from six collaborating organizations in Finland in the spring of 2024. In total, we conducted 54 interviews and later had workshops with the organizations that represented fields such as urban planning, media and communications, IT services and consulting, forestry and paper, and one city organization. Hence, these organizations covered a large spectrum of Finnish working life, but obviously not all sectors, as in our surveys. With the interviews and workshops, we were interested in hearing workers' and organizations' perspectives on the changes brought by AI, and we saw rather big leaps from the original interviews conducted in spring 2024 to the workshops implemented in spring 2025.

Intelligent technologies were also covered in our *Social Media at Work Longitudinal Survey* (*WorkSome*) that targeted Finnish employees ($N =$

1817) starting in mid-March 2019. These data were collected biannually and currently cover 14 time points from the same participants. The study was designed by our research groups, but Norstat handled the data collection. The data are representative of Finnish workers in terms of sociodemographic variables and geographical area (Oksa et al., 2021). The *WorkSome* survey has the major strength of having started before the COVID-19 pandemic. In Finland, the entire working life took a major digital leap during COVID-19 (Oksanen et al., 2021), and remote working practices permanently changed the working landscape (Pekkala et al., 2025). The rapid rise of AI technologies represents another major change during the follow-up period of the survey, during which the survey items were updated. Response rates have been very high considering the survey collection period spanning 6 years. For example, in total, 748 responded to the latest T14 survey in September–November 2025. This marked 41 % of the original T1 survey respondents.

The *Self and Technology* Project survey data sets mark the third data utilized in this book. The *Self and Technology EU Six-country Longitudinal Survey* (*SelfTech-EU-6*) surveys started in autumn 2022 in Finland (N = 1541), France (N = 1561), Germany (N = 1529), Ireland (N = 1112), Italy (N = 1530), and Poland (N = 1533). These samples closely align with Eurostat's 2022 data regarding the gender and age distributions of the populations of the respective countries within the 18–75-year age range (Heiskari et al., 2025). The *SelfTech-EU-6* surveys were collected annually until autumn 2025, targeting the 18- to 75-year-old population. The last wave (T4) was finalized in November 2025 and covered 45 % (n = 3997) of the original T1 respondents (N = 8806). Norstat collected these surveys, but the study was designed by Atte Oksanen and his research group. These surveys have a large variety of questions concerning the use of technologies in everyday life. The survey was designed from a social–psychological perspective. It also covers necessary additions to the newest technologies used. We extended the Self and Technology surveys to the Americas, Africa, Asia, and Oceania. These *Self and Technology Global Extended Six-country Survey* (*SelfTech-GE-6*) surveys were collected from 18–75-year-olds in Australia (N = 1487), Brazil (N = 1512), Japan (N = 1569), Portugal (N = 1522), South Africa (N = 1530), and the USA (N = 1543) in 2024. The survey questionnaire was identical to the *SelfTech-EU-6* survey. Data collection was handled by Dynata in October 2024.

Overall, our data, despite having a focus on Finland and Europe, cover six continents and a diverse array of cultural, economic, and technological environments. The countries were selected to reflect distinct cultural regions globally (Inglehart & Oyserman, 2004; Inglehart & Welzel, 2005; World Values Survey, 2023) and varying levels of digital infrastructure, educational systems, and policy focus on AI adoption. Considering the global AI race, we feel it is important to have a cross-national perspective on the topic. Our key strength involves, however, the longitudinal data and the possibility of following the changes in population in each country.

The Structure of the Book

Our book is structured into seven chapters. This chapter sets the stage by introducing the central theme: how AI is reshaping workplaces.

Chapter 2 provides an overview of the current AI disruption, placing it in a historical context. We review foundational research on technological change and the history of workplace innovation, situating current developments within a larger trajectory of historical shifts in how work has been organized and conducted. We end with the most recent developments.

Chapter 3 covers empirical evidence concerning the rapid diffusion of AI technologies across the globe. We analyze patterns of use, attitudes, and affective responses to AI. New technologies have always caused concerns and worries among people. Also, currently, public discourse around AI in the workplace frequently leans toward pessimism and fear-based narratives. We aim to cover the roots of these affective reactions and show how attitudes toward technologies play a significant role in their adoption and potential gains. This chapter relies on empirical evidence gained from our surveys and considers future expectations of AI.

Chapter 4 provides new, necessary evidence on how workers across different sectors and roles experience AI in relation to their professional identities. To date, the role of the self has been largely overlooked in discussions of AI-driven disruptions. The current emergence of AI places significant stress on worker identity, especially in fields that have been previously dominated by human work only. The most profound changes occur when AI is not simply a tool but rather replaces the work previously conducted solely or mostly by humans. AI potentially challenges how individuals perceive themselves and their professional identities. We examine how AI-related identity threats emerge, who is most likely to experience them, and how these threats relate to stress and strain over time. The chapter situates AI-related stress within the broader literature on technostress and shows that identity threats constitute a central psychological pathway through which AI intensifies strain. In addition, we introduce coping resources that can mitigate these effects.

Chapter 5 focuses on AI learning readiness self-efficacy as a central psychological resource shaping how workers adapt to AI-driven change. Moving beyond stress and threat, this chapter examines how confidence in one's ability to use and learn AI technologies relates to work engagement and well-being. We first report cross-national patterns of work engagement and show how engagement is associated with positive experiences of AI use. The chapter then positions self-efficacy as a key mechanism through which AI can become a resource at work. Self-efficacy is conceptualized as workers' beliefs in their capacity to effectively perform tasks and solve problems in AI-augmented environments. As AI adoption increasingly requires employees to experiment, learn, and adapt with limited guidance, self-efficacy emerges as a crucial factor supporting engagement, motivation, and psychological resilience.

Chapter 6 looks at future workers beyond psychological adaptation to the change. We consider what remains uniquely human in the workplace in the age of AI, with particular attention to the implications of AI on autonomy, creativity, and innovation. We discuss how human–AI collaboration can augment creative intelligence, and what institutional and leadership conditions are needed to protect human value and creativity in increasingly automated work settings. We consider organizational factors and leadership as central and stress the importance of creating supportive spaces for innovation and experimentation that can make change more inclusive and successful. We acknowledge that not all workers will be able or willing to adapt in the same way. For some, alternative pathways may involve transitioning to a new career, pursuing further education, or even exiting the workforce. Although some jobs will disappear and new ones will arise, many workers will not be replaced but augmented.

Chapter 7 concludes the book by providing key lessons learned from our research and analysis of workers in the age of AI. We present both theoretical and empirical implications as well as practical implications for workplaces and policies. The future of work raises ethical questions that we address by outlining principles for an ethical and resilient working life. This perspective highlights the need to ensure that human-centered AI design accounts for social and economic inequalities and fosters inclusive futures across sectors and worker populations. This requires mutual effort; the direction and consequences of AI-driven change are currently not determined by technology alone but by the actors who design, deploy, and distribute the systems. Technology firms, organizations, and policymakers largely decide how AI is integrated into work and whose interests are prioritized. Going forward, societal impacts remain conditional on collective choices about regulation and participation. This concluding chapter also invites readers to imagine new ways of collaboration, creativity, and meaning in work that elevate human potential rather than simply accommodate technological change.

References

Acemoglu, D., & Restrepo, P. (2018). Artificial intelligence, automation, and work. In A. Agrawal, J. Gans, & A. Goldfarb (Eds.), *The economics of artificial intelligence: An agenda* (pp. 197–236). University of Chicago Press.

Bankins, S., Ocampo, A. C., Marrone, M., Restubog, S. L. D., & Woo, S. E. (2024). A multilevel review of artificial intelligence in organizations: Implications for organizational behavior research and practice. *Journal of Organizational Behavior, 45*(2), 159–182. https://doi.org/10.1002/job.2735

Heiskari, M., Celuch, M., Koivula, A., Savolainen, I., & Oksanen, A. (2025). Technological identity and basic psychological needs in the use of new technologies: A two-wave cross-national survey study. *International Journal of Information Management, 84*(October), 102926. https://doi.org/10.1016/j.ijinfomgt.2025.102926

Horodyski, P. (2023). Recruiter's perception of artificial intelligence (AI)-based tools in recruitment. *Computers in Human Behavior Reports, 10*(May), 100298. https://doi.org/10.1016/j.chbr.2023.100298

Inglehart, R., & Oyserman, D. (2004). Individualism, autonomy, self-expression: The human development syndrome. In H. Vinken, J. Soeters, & P. Ester (Eds.), *Comparing cultures: Dimensions of culture in a comparative perspective* (pp. 73–96). Brill. https://doi.org/10.1163/9789047412977_008

Inglehart, R., & Welzel, C. (2005). *Modernization, cultural change and democracy: The human development sequence*. Cambridge University Press.

Kambur, E., & Akar, C. (2022). Human resource developments with the touch of artificial intelligence: A scale development study. *International Journal of Manpower, 43*(1), 168–205. https://doi.org/10.1108/IJM-04-2021-0216

López Jiménez, E. A., & Ouariachi, T. (2021). An exploration of the impact of artificial intelligence (AI) and automation for communication professionals. *Journal of Information, Communication and Ethics in Society, 19*(2), 249–267. https://doi.org/10.1108/JICES-03-2020-0034

Oksa, R., Kaakinen, M., Savela, N., Ellonen, N., & Oksanen, A. (2021). Professional social media usage: Work engagement perspective. *New Media & Society, 23*(8), 2303–2326. https://doi.org/10.1177/1461444820921938

Oksanen, A., Oksa, R., Savela, N., Mantere, E., Savolainen, I., & Kaakinen, M. (2021). COVID-19 crisis and digital stressors at work: A nationwide longitudinal study. *Computers in Human Behavior, 122*(September), 106853. https://doi.org/10.1016/j.chb.2021.106853

Pekkala, K., Oksa, R., & Oksanen, A. (2025). Sense of community, social support and social media use in post-pandemic world of work. *Behaviour & Information Technology, 44*(16), 4082–4095. https://doi.org/10.1080/0144929X.2025.2461726

Russell, S., & Norvig, P. (2021). *Artificial intelligence: A modern approach* (4th ed.). Pearson.

Sapkota, R., Roumeliotis, K. I., & Karkee, M. (2025). AI agents vs. agentic AI: A conceptual taxonomy, applications and challenges. *Information Fusion, 126*(Part B, February), 103599. https://doi.org/10.1016/j.inffus.2025.103599

Savolainen, I., Ylinen, L., Grönroos, R., & Oksanen, A. (2026). AI transformation in working life: A systematic review of usage and attitudes towards AI among workers. *Digital Business, 6*(1), 100162. https://doi.org/10.1016/j.digbus.2025.100162

Stern, J. (2025, December 18). We let AI run our office vending machine. It lost hundreds of dollars. *The Wall Street Journal.* https://www.wsj.com/tech/ai/anthropic-claude-ai-vending-machine-agent-b7e84e34

Tully, S. M., Longoni, C., & Appel, G. (2025). Lower artificial intelligence literacy predicts greater AI receptivity. *Journal of Marketing, 89*(5), 1–20. https://doi.org/10.1177/00222429251314491

Wang, X., Lin, X., & Shao, B. (2023). Artificial intelligence changes the way we work: A close look at innovating with chatbots. *Journal of the Association for Information Science and Technology, 74*(3), 339–353. https://doi.org/10.1002/asi.24621

World Values Survey. (2023). Findings and insights—Inglehart–Welzel cultural map. https://www.worldvaluessurvey.org/WVSContents.jsp?CMSID=findings

Zúñiga, N., Burton, S. D., Blancato, F., & Carr, M. (2024). The geopolitics of technology standards: Historical context for US, EU and Chinese approaches. *International Affairs, 100*(4), 1635–1652. https://doi.org/10.1093/ia/iiae124

CHAPTER 2

Laying the Foundations of Automated Work

Abstract Innovation thrives on human creativity and imagination. Today's technological advancements are the result of decades of development, each innovation building upon the last. In this chapter, we lay the foundation for understanding today's AI applications by tracing the history of technological development. We begin with early mechanical machines and proceed to robotization, automation, and digitalization, culminating in the current era of AI approaching full bloom. We consider this evolution from the perspective of workers, highlighting how technological advancement and digitalization have transformed work since the introduction of the first calculators. While earlier technological and digital change unfolded gradually over more than a century following the Industrial Revolution, today's workforce is experiencing an AI-driven transformation that has unfolded within just a few years. We conclude by exploring how individuals and organizations navigate this rapid pace of change and what possibilities may lie ahead.

Keywords History • Work • Automation • Robots • Digitalization • Artificial intelligence

> *Our ignorance of history leads us to misjudge our own time.* Gustave Flaubert in a letter to George Sand, dated September 8, 1871 (Flaubert, 1930, p. 283).

A. Oksanen, I. Savolainen, *AI Disruption at Work*, Palgrave Advances in Work and Organizational Psychology,
https://doi.org/10.1007/978-3-032-35207-1_2

The ignorance of history is common in technological disruptions. Our everyday world is focused on daily events, and the worlds of media and social media consistently push new information our way, ensuring hype with the most recent events in the world. It is very human to forget history. Some years ago, when researchers in the social sciences and philosophy at Tampere University were engaged in a new project on social robots, the fancy word of robotization popped up and was flavored with novelty. "What do you mean by new?" asked the first author of this book, Atte Oksanen, who had spent his childhood summers in the 1980s and early 1990s traveling across Finland, Sweden, and Europe to see industrial automation lines due to his father's job as an automation design engineer.

In the world of computing, almost nothing is entirely new. The first home computers were introduced over 50 years ago, with Altair 8000 released in the beginning of 1975 and leading the way to the success of companies like Commodore, Atari, and Apple in the 1980s (O'Regan, 2012). Computers became popular among offices in the 1970s, but they were already used in the late 1940s (Land, 2000). However, considering the automation of office work, mechanical calculators were commonly used in the late nineteenth century and the early twentieth century (Heller, 2016). French mathematician Blaise Pascal invented the first operational calculator in 1642 (Kistermann, 1998; O'Regan, 2012), but in offices, calculators were a novelty in the late nineteenth century.

The transition from calculating humans to machines was slow, as early electronic computers were expensive and scarce. Their emergence elicited both enthusiasm and concern, as some clerks expressed worry about deskilling or loss of status, but others welcomed new technologies such as calculators and typewriters as symbols of progress (Heller, 2016). Automation has become particularly useful in sectors requiring a high and accurate applied math skillset, such as finance, insurance, engineering, universities, and aerospace. With the introduction of electronic computers, human workers initially worked alongside the computer, checking the work and programming. Eventually, many of these skilled workers became the first computer programmers.

Historical discussions and debates about technologies sound familiar today. What has changed are the devices or solutions considered to be the newest technologies. For late nineteenth-century clerks in London, these were calculators and typewriters; for us, they are different AI technologies. In this chapter, we consider the historical roots of the current AI transformation. We first provide a small excursion to the early automation and robotization, before focusing on the more recent digitalization, and finally considering the ongoing developments with AI technologies.

Rise of the Machines: From Automation to Robotization

The current AI disruption unfolds in a historical context that can be traced back to the First Industrial Revolution (Ashton, 1997) or the first age of machines (Brynjolfsson & McAfee, 2014). The First Industrial Revolution started in Britain in the late eighteenth century and spread to Europe and the United States in the early nineteenth century. Key developments involved the steam engine, iron production, and factory-based organization of work. Importantly, the textile industry was mechanized. Luddites, named after symbolic movement leader Ned Ludd, started to resist the change in response to the threat the machines posed to their trade (Jones, 2013). Luddism was essentially a social movement aiming to protect the interests of skilled workers in the absence of regulations protecting them (Hobsbawm, 1952).

The age of automation started long after the Luddites and was enabled by the beginning of the Second Industrial Revolution in the 1870s. It involved the adoption of electricity, oil, and gas. Large-scale standardized production—in other words, Fordism, derived from Ford's automobile factories—marked this change. In addition, the word automation was commonly used in the 1940s (Mair, 1993, p. 319). The word derives from the Greek automatos, which means acting independently. The word automaton (plural automata) had been used since the Greeks and referred to a self-operating machine. Whereas the First Industrial Revolution was characterized by the replacement of human and animal muscles with inanimate power in work, such as textile production and transport, the Second Industrial Revolution reorganized physical production through electrification and the mass production it enabled.

Following these industrial revolutions, businesses grew, and the nature of work increasingly shifted from predominantly manual labor toward administrative, documenting, and record-keeping tasks (Rotella, 1981). Office work required specialized roles and became more structured. From the late nineteenth century to the turn of the twentieth century, office jobs and work related to handling information began to change, as early office machines were introduced and gradually implemented. In the

United States, particularly in the 1970s, automation and technological changes were rapid (Autor, 2015). These developments simplified the tasks of clerical workers and reduced labor-intensive manual effort, and the new skills required to operate new technologies were often acquired with relative ease. For instance, clerical workers with experience using traditional office equipment were able to adapt quickly to new electric typewriters.

Early digital computing, in contrast, required a novel set of skills and created a demand for technical personnel who could take on tasks overseeing and operating these machines. As a result, computers reduced the importance of some traditional clerical skills, such as manual filing, and reshaped the roles of workers in charge of record keeping (International Labour Office, 1960). The advantages of computers in office work were immense, increasing productivity and lowering the unit cost of clerical output. This, in turn, enabled the expansion of clerical labor (Rotella, 1981). Early computer systems could process routine tasks, such as payroll and accounting, at a much higher speed and with fewer errors than a manual laborer.

Advances in computing have enabled increasingly specialized forms of technological progress. During the 1960s and 1970s, interest grew in combining analog and digital computing. Programmable automation promised improvements in several core aspects of manufacturing: efficiency, flexibility, coordination, and information flow (Dilts et al., 1991). The application of computerized techniques to control production tools, process manufacturing data, and plan and design production processes enabled more efficient manufacturing and a higher degree of organizational control. While computerization and programmable automation significantly transformed production control and information processing, later technological developments extended automation to the execution of physical tasks, paving the way for industrial robotization.

The development of robots marked a logical next step in industrial automation. The word "robot" originates from the Czech word *robota* and was popularized by Karel Čapek's 1921 play *R.U.R.* (Rossum's Universal Robots), which was used to describe artificial workers (Jordan, 2019). The word refers to "forced labor." Čapek himself was critical of unchecked science and technological progress. The play reflects this skepticism and is widely interpreted as a critique of mechanization and its potential to dehumanize both workers and society more broadly

(Christoforou & Müller, 2016). Although Čapek's skepticism toward mechanization was not completely unwarranted, his play coined a term that would describe an entire industry and a trajectory of technological development.

Industrial robotization represents a stage of automation in which computerized control systems are coupled with machines capable of performing physical tasks in production environments (Grau et al., 2020). Among the significant achievements of industrial robotization are increased precision and improved worker safety, as automation has reduced human exposure to dangerous tasks. The development of industrial robots spans from the 1950s to the present. The first three generations of industrial robots can be broadly categorized into: (1) programmable machines that execute preset tasks without adjusting how the action is performed; (2) programmable machines with limited self-adaptive capabilities and some ability to detect external cues from the environment; and (3) programmable machines equipped with more advanced interfaces, partial self-programming features, and greater interaction with both operators and their surroundings. Together, these three generations largely characterize industrial robots up to the late 1990s. From 2000 onward, the newly developed robots are often described as the fourth generation, characterized by high-level intelligent capabilities, such as logical reasoning, deep learning, collaborative operation, and the ability to perform advanced computations (Gasparetto & Scalera, 2019; Grau et al., 2020).

As we move into a new era of AI implementation, increasingly advanced opportunities are emerging in robotics. Already in Čapek's *R.U.R.* in the 1920s, robots were imagined as artificial workers designed to take over human labor, promising efficiency and convenience. At the same time, they raised uneasiness and concern about dehumanization and control. Today, over 100 years later, the same sentiments are reflected in the adoption of AI. It is expanding the possibilities of robotics further, enabling them to perform a wider range of tasks, adopt more human-like characteristics, and reshape how humans interact with automated systems.

Digitally Transformed Work

When thinking about the automation of labor and offices, it is easy to picture workers in front of computers or rows of robots performing assembly line tasks. Robotics and similar emerging technologies are visible in manifestations of automation. However, the advancement that followed was often less obvious to the naked eye and reflected a broader societal and organizational shift, commonly described as digital transformation. Digitalization refers to the adoption of digital technologies, whereas digital transformation involves deeper organizational change, including new workflows, reconfigured roles, and data-driven decision-making (Gradillas & Thomas, 2025). For example, organizations increasingly replaced traditional and fragmented processes with integrated digital platforms that allowed information to flow in real time across departments, enabling coordination, monitoring, and automation at scale. Everyday examples include banks shifting from paper statements to digital records and retailers offering digital receipts instead of printed slips.

Digitalization gained momentum during the 1980s. The decade marked the emergence of personal computers (PCs). During this time, computers were primarily used for basic data functions, including entering, storing, processing, and printing information. Firms such as IBM and Apple played a central role in bringing computing into everyday use and expanding access beyond specialized institutional settings (Campbell-Kelly et al., 2023; Dornberger et al., 2018). As research in information and knowledge management developed, more focus was placed on how raw data could be organized and transformed into information and knowledge. At the same time, the growing availability of computers in workplaces and households has led to an increase in the amount of data generated. This created a need for data storage infrastructures, such as databases and warehouses, but it also intensified organizations' concerns about managing records (Dornberger et al., 2018; Inmon et al., 2008).

The spread of PCs and data infrastructures altered organizational processes as well as the composition of the work itself. This would naturally lead to the following question: How did automation and digitalization affect subsequent employment? Considering decades of automation and more recent developments in robotization and digitalization, Autor (2015) analyzed twentieth-century trends in job markets. He concluded that although technological development has indeed replaced jobs, it did not replace work. Historically, automation has increased productivity and demand, thus providing a new demand for employment. Nonroutine tasks are still difficult to completely automate, and human workers also possess a lot of tacit knowledge; this entails that they know more than they can tell. Automation, however, has driven labor market polarization. This has meant that employment has grown at the top in high-skilled and cognitively demanding jobs over the last decades.

With the rise of networking and the internet, these shifts would be accelerated, further transforming both the organization of work and the demand for different types of new skills. The diffusion of the internet accelerated during the 1990s, marking a major shift in how information was created, shared, and accessed. A key turning point came in 1991 when Tim Berners-Lee introduced the World Wide Web, and the first website was published (Kleinrock, 2010; Leiner et al., 1997). Although its origins lay in earlier research projects, such as the Advanced Research Projects Agency Network (ARPANET) (Abbate, 2000), the 1990s marked the decade when the internet became a mass technology. This made it significantly easier to publish, link, and browse information through a standardized web-based interface. This development transformed how information is circulated and how people consume knowledge in their everyday lives and work. More broadly, the internet is often described as a landmark example of the achievements made possible by long-term investment in research and information infrastructure (Leiner et al., 2009).

The significance of the internet does not solely pertain to improved efficiency in information access and dissemination. Its impacts are widely felt at both the societal and individual levels. In the late 1990s and early 2000s, when going to the internet still required several steps, getting to a computer and waiting a few minutes to connect, it was difficult to imagine the scale of connectivity and networking that would follow. Sociologist Manuel Castells (2004, 2020) has argued that contemporary society is increasingly organized as a network society. In this social structure, the most influential economic, political, and cultural processes operate through digitally mediated networks rather than primarily through industrial structures. Generating and processing information, and connecting to global networks produce an informational economy that reconfigures power and inequality; network inclusion enables opportunity and influence, while exclusion can intensify marginalization (Castells, 2023; van Dijk, 2020).

What followed the spread of networked connectivity was not simply more information but new ways of structuring and supervising work through software. The 2000s saw the rise of platforms and enterprise systems that organized and monitored work processes. In particular, digital platforms and enterprise systems, such as enterprise resource planning and workflow management tools, integrated business functions across organizations and enabled more standardized oversight and coordination (Acs et al., 2021; Gupta & Kohli, 2006). In the 2010s, this logic intensified through datafication and algorithmic systems, as growing volumes of digital data increasingly informed decision-making, performance evaluation, and automated aspects of control (Bonina et al., 2021; Gawer, 2022). Together, these developments marked a progression from digital support systems toward the data-driven execution of work, laying the foundation for the emergence of AI-driven workflows and management. By the early 2020s, digital platforms and datafication had created conditions that supported the rapid diffusion of AI systems across organizational settings.

AI Approaching Full Bloom

Today's technological context looks quite different from the pre-2020 era. AI has shifted from a background technology to a visible presence across popular culture, media, and everyday work. AI systems are now widely accessible and used by millions, reaching what can be described as the era of AI in full bloom. Although today's AI boom may appear sudden in the prominence of AI tools, its rapid adoption reflects the convergence of multiple long-term trends enabled by decades of technological advancements and sustained investment in digital infrastructures and innovation. Leading technology firms, including Microsoft, Alphabet (Google), Meta, Apple, and Amazon, continue to make large-scale investments in AI technology and development. Beyond consumer- and platform-based AI, enterprise software providers such as IBM, Oracle, and SAP have also expanded through substantial AI investments, particularly in analytics, automation, and business process integration.

AI's potential has been much discussed, and there have been high-profile demonstrations of its capabilities over the years, which have helped make even abstract advances visible, better understood, and tangible to a wider audience. One such defining moment was in 2016 when DeepMind's AlphaGo defeated the reigning human champion in the game of Go. AlphaGo combines deep learning, reinforcement learning, and large-scale computing. Before this, success in Go had been considered a unique human achievement, requiring intuition, strategic reasoning, and the ability to navigate the game, all the while thinking about the vast possible moves ahead. AlphaGo's victory, therefore, marked more than a technical milestone in machine sophistication; it signposted that learning-based AI systems could outperform humans in complex and nonroutine decision-making tasks. What was a moment of entertaining engagement between a human and a machine, the game of Go turned out to be a turning point that transformed into broader real-world applications of AI and challenged existing assumptions about what is possible.

A decisive technical breakthrough underpinning the current success of AI is the introduction of transformer architecture. It helps explain how contemporary AI systems expanded in scope and became more general purpose. The transformer was first presented in the 2017 paper *"Attention Is All You Need"* (Vaswani et al., 2017). Transformers process sequential data by computing relationships between all tokens simultaneously through a mechanism called self-attention. This enables models to capture relationships, context, and meaning across vast amounts of data. This shift proved critical for scaling AI systems and moving beyond narrow, task-specific applications. Transformers allow AI systems to engage directly with different types of material (e.g., text or images), making it possible to augment or automate tasks, including writing, summarizing, programming, and analysis (Khan et al., 2022). By learning patterns from large-scale data, transformer-based models can be generalized across varied tasks and domains. Handling such large data sets was made possible by advances in hardware, particularly the use of GPUs as well as by the expansion of cloud-based computing infrastructures. Transformer technology also enabled the development of LLMs on which current GenAI applications, such as ChatGPT, Claude, and Gemini, are based. In this sense, transformer architecture laid the foundation for AI to move from a largely invisible background infrastructure to an active and visible participant in everyday work processes.

The new era of AI that we live in today was marked by the release of OpenAI's ChatGPT in November 2022. Its global competitors followed soon after. For example, Gemini by Google was originally released as Bard in March 2023. Copilot is integrated into the Microsoft ecosystem and is widely utilized, especially in enterprises. Anthropic's Claude was released in March 2023. Among European alternatives, Mistral's first model was released in September 2023. Among Chinese solutions, DeepSeek has also attracted global users. ChatGPT was an instant hit, and it took only two months to reach 100 million users (Hu, 2023). The pace of reaching 100 million users was fast, even in the context of the internet. For example, it took Facebook about four years to reach 100 million users after its release in 2004, after which Instagram reached the same figure in two years and

TikTok in nine months. Historically, the diffusion of new technologies has been much slower. It took the World Wide Web most of the 1990s to reach similar figures.

An important feature of the development of AI is that it extends beyond GenAI and LLMs. AI systems are already embedded in the background of many work processes, often operating invisibly in areas such as optimization, prediction, and decision support. Users may not always know that they are working with AI. GenAI, however, represents the most visible, approachable, and user-friendly part of the current AI landscape. One of its key innovations lies in the user interface, which helps explain why the diffusion of GenAI tools, such as ChatGPT, has been so rapid. Before ChatGPT, AI tools were available but not as easy to use or relevant for many. Now, the advantage of conversational AI interfaces is that anyone can use them. They are intuitive and easy to use, with tremendous flexibility in how to apply them. In addition, they do not have language barriers like standard internet search engines, in which you might have gotten a better answer by doing your search in the right language. Users could, for example, rely on their own language instead of using English or other languages that might provide more information. At the same time, intensified global competition among technology companies has made GenAI tools widely accessible through free versions or relatively affordable subscription models. Together, these developments have substantially lowered barriers to access and use.

During the 2020s, AI development was both rapid and strongly driven by large-scale investments. Particularly following the introduction of GenAI tools, these developments reshaped how policymakers, organizations, and the wider public viewed AI's role across different areas of life, including work and society, more broadly. In organizational contexts, AI tools are increasingly utilized. They support routine tasks and decision-making, which in turn accelerate experimentation and investment across industries (Babina et al., 2024). As a result, AI has moved decisively from a background technology embedded in infrastructures and expert systems to a visible, everyday tool directly encountered by a broad range of users. Development of AI has continued, and agentic AI systems increasingly move beyond generating outputs toward executing tasks and coordinating complex workflows (Hughes et al., 2025; Sapkota et al., 2025).

Conclusion: All Roads Lead to AI

The developments traced in this chapter suggest that many of the major technological, organizational, and societal trajectories of recent decades now converge and culminate in AI. The process of automation and digitalization of work has taken decades, and early historical examples of automation of work exist. Starting with mechanization, automation, and robotization, the industrial transformation of working life has progressively shifted ways of working and labor markets. Each historical development has been groundbreaking and significant in its time, improving productivity and safety but also redefining work, skills, occupational boundaries, and organizational opportunities and control. Building on foundations, such as mechanical power in factories, the diffusion of personal computers in homes and offices, and industrial robots in manufacturing, AI has fully blossomed. Thus, progress itself is not a novelty. Rather, when it comes to today's AI landscape, the pace of change enabled by quick diffusion and lowered barriers to use has been unparalleled.

From a historical perspective, any major technological development has often been experienced by the people of the time as disruptive, transformative, or even unsettling. At the same time, each has been described as a step toward progress, promising efficiency, safety, or altogether better ways of working. As history has shown, technological development rarely results in the simple replacement of human labor. Instead, it translates into the development of new tasks and skills, and the reshaping autonomy and control. Whereas productivity gains have been a major motivator for altering ways of working with technology, they have not been achieved through machines or technology alone. Workers' ability to adapt, experiment, and reskill has been a crucial factor. The characteristics of today's AI boom follow similar trajectories. It enters the workplace at a rapid pace, requiring uptake and experimentation from workers. It is also clear that upskilling is necessary, especially in certain fields, such as administration, health care, or software.

Contemporary discussions on AI are also increasingly framed by the prospect of artificial general intelligence (AGI). It is understood as a form of AI capable of general and flexible intelligence, parallel to a well-educated individual (Hendrycks et al., 2025), with the potential to exceed human performance in most tasks (Bikkasani, 2025). Although AGI has not yet been realized, similar future-oriented visions have been part of prior technological developments, influencing what to expect and how people anticipate new changes. In this sense, AGI provides a valuable forward-looking narrative that likely impacts responses to present-day AI. Like earlier technologies, AI provokes both optimism and anxiety and is seen as having the capacity to both advance work practices and threaten established ways of working and living. The progress of AI is the culmination of a longer historical process of digitalization and automation, setting the stage for changing attitudes, expectations, and forms of use, which are examined in the next chapter.

References

Abbate, J. (2000). *Inventing the internet*. MIT Press.

Acs, Z. J., Song, A. K., Szerb, L., Audretsch, D. B., & Komlósi, É. (2021). The evolution of the global digital platform economy: 1971–2021. *Small Business Economics, 57*(4), 1629–1659. https://doi.org/10.1007/s11187-021-00561-x

Ashton, T. S. (1997). *The Industrial Revolution 1760–1830*. Oxford University Press.

Autor, D. H. (2015). Why are there still so many jobs? The history and future of workplace automation. *Journal of Economic Perspectives, 29*(3), 3–30. https://doi.org/10.1257/jep.29.3.3

Babina, T., Fedyk, A., He, A., & Hodson, J. (2024). Artificial intelligence, firm growth, and product innovation. *Journal of Financial Economics, 151*, 103745. https://doi.org/10.1016/j.jfineco.2023.103745

Bikkasani, D. C. (2025). Navigating artificial general intelligence (AGI): Societal implications, ethical considerations, and governance strategies. *AI and Ethics, 5*(3), 2021–2036. https://doi.org/10.1007/s43681-024-00642-z

Bonina, C., Koskinen, K., Eaton, B., & Gawer, A. (2021). Digital platforms for development: Foundations and research agenda. *Information Systems Journal, 31*(6), 869–902. https://doi.org/10.1111/isj.12326

Brynjolfsson, E., & McAfee, A. (2014). *The second machine age: Work, progress, and prosperity in a time of brilliant technologies*. W. W. Norton & Company.

Campbell-Kelly, M., Aspray, W. F., Yost, J. R., Tinn, H., & Díaz, G. C. (2023). Broadening the appeal. In M. Campbell-Kelly, W. F. Aspray, J. R. Yost, H. Tinn, G. C. Díaz, & N. Ensmenger (Eds.), *Computer: A history of the information machine*. Routledge. https://doi.org/10.4324/9781003263272

Castells, M. (Ed.). (2004). *The network society*. Edward Elgar Publishing. https://doi.org/10.4337/9781845421663

Castells, M. (2020). The information city, the new economy, and the network society. In R. Blom, E. Karvonen, H. Melin, K. Nordenstreng, E. Puoskari,

F. Webster, & P. F. Webster (Eds.), *The information society reader* (pp. 150–164). Routledge.

Castells, M. (2023). The network society revisited. *American Behavioral Scientist, 67*(7), 940–946. https://doi.org/10.1177/00027642221092803

Christoforou, E. G., & Müller, A. (2016). RUR revisited: Perspectives and reflections on modern robotics. *International Journal of Social Robotics, 8*(2), 237–246. https://doi.org/10.1007/s12369-015-0327-6

Dilts, D. M., Boyd, N. P., & Whorms, H. H. (1991). The evolution of control architectures for automated manufacturing systems. *Journal of Manufacturing Systems, 10*(1), 79–93. https://doi.org/10.1016/0278-6125(91)90049-8

Dornberger, R., Inglese, T., Korkut, S., & Zhong, V. J. (2018). Digitalization: Yesterday, today and tomorrow. In R. Dornberger (Ed.), *Business information systems and technology 4.0: New trends in the age of digital change* (pp. 1–11). Springer International Publishing. https://doi.org/10.1007/978-3-319-74322-6_1

Flaubert, G. (1930). *Oeuvres Completes De Gustave Flaubert: Correspondance, Sixième Serie (1869–1872)*, (Vol. 6). [The complete works of Gustave Flaubert]. Louis Conard.

Gasparetto, A., & Scalera, L. (2019). A brief history of industrial robotics in the 20th century. *Advances in Historical Studies, 8*, 24–35. https://doi.org/10.4236/ahs.2019.81002

Gawer, A. (2022). Digital platforms and ecosystems: Remarks on the dominant organizational forms of the digital age. *Innovation, 24*(1), 110–124. https://doi.org/10.1080/14479338.2021.1965888

Gradillas, M., & Thomas, L. D. (2025). Distinguishing digitization and digitalization: A systematic review and conceptual framework. *Journal of Product Innovation Management, 42*(1), 112–143. https://doi.org/10.1111/jpim.12690

Grau, A., Indri, M., Bello, L. L., & Sauter, T. (2020). Robots in industry: The past, present, and future of a growing collaboration with humans. *IEEE Industrial Electronics Magazine, 15*(1), 50–61. https://doi.org/10.1109/MIE.2020.3008136

Gupta, M., & Kohli, A. (2006). Enterprise resource planning systems and its implications for operations function. *Technovation, 26*(5–6), 687–696. https://doi.org/10.1016/j.technovation.2004.10.005

Heller, M. (2016). *London clerical workers, 1880–1914: Development of the labour market. Routledge.* https://doi.org/10.4324/9781315655987

Hendrycks, D., Song, D., Szegedy, C., Lee, H., Gal, Y., Brynjolfsson, E., Li, S., Zou, A., Levine, L., Han, B., Fu, J., Liu, Z., Shin, J., Lee, K., Mazeika, M., Phan, L., Ingebretsen, G., Khoja, A., Xie, C., … & Bengio, Y. (2025). A definition of AGI. arXiv preprint. https://arxiv.org/abs/2510.18212. https://doi.org/10.48550/arXiv.2510.18212

Hobsbawm, E. J. (1952). The machine breakers. *Past & Present, 1*, 57–70. https://www.jstor.org/stable/649989.

Hu, K. (2023, February 2). ChatGPT sets record for fastest-growing user base—Analyst note. *Reuters*. https://www.reuters.com/technology/chatgpt-sets-record-fastest-growing-user-base-analyst-note-2023-02-01/.

Hughes, L., Dwivedi, Y. K., Malik, T., Shawosh, M., Albashrawi, M. A., Jeon, I., et al. (2025). AI agents and agentic systems: A multi-expert analysis. *Journal of Computer Information Systems, 65*(4), 489–517. https://doi.org/10.1080/08874417.2025.2483832

Inmon, W. H., Strauss, D., & Neushloss, G. (2008). A brief history of data warehousing and first-generation data warehouses. In W. H. Inmon, D. Strauss, & G. Neushloss (Eds.), *DW 2.0: The architecture for the next generation of data warehousing* (pp. 1–22). Morgan Kaufmann Publishers, Elsevier.

International Labour Office. (1960). Effects of mechanisation and automation in offices; II. *International Labour Review, 81*(3), 255–273.

Jones, S. E. (2013). *Against technology: From the Luddites to neo-Luddism*. Routledge.

Jordan, J. M. (2019). The Czech play that gave us the word "robot." *The MIT Press Reader*. https://thereader.mitpress.mit.edu/origin-word-robot-rur/

Khan, S., Naseer, M., Hayat, M., Zamir, S. W., Khan, F. S., & Shah, M. (2022). Transformers in vision: A survey. *ACM Computing Surveys (CSUR), 54*(10s), 1–41. https://doi.org/10.1145/3505244

Kistermann, F. W. (1998). Blaise Pascal's adding machine: New findings and conclusions. *IEEE Annals of the History of Computing, 20*(1), 69–76. https://doi.org/10.1109/85.646211

Kleinrock, L. (2010). An early history of the internet [History of communications]. *IEEE Communications Magazine, 48*(8), 26–36. https://doi.org/10.1109/MCOM.2010.5534584

Land, F. (2000). The First Business Computer: A case study in user-driven innovation. *IEEE Annals of the History of Computing, 22*(3), 16–26. https://doi.org/10.1109/85.859523

Leiner, B. M., Cerf, V. G., Clark, D. D., Kahn, R. E., Kleinrock, L., Lynch, D. C., Postel, J., Roberts, L. G., & Wolff, S. (2009). A brief history of the internet. *ACM SIGCOMM Computer Communication Review, 39*(5), 22–31. https://doi.org/10.1145/1629607.1629613

Leiner, B. M., Cerf, V. G., Clark, D. D., Kahn, R. E., Kleinrock, L., Lynch, D. C., Postel, J., Roberts, L. G., & Wolff, S. S. (1997). The past and future history of the internet. *Communications of the ACM, 40*(2), 102–108. https://doi.org/10.1145/253671.253741

Mair, G. (1993). Elements of automation. In G. Mair (Ed.), *Mastering manufacturing* (pp. 319–334). Macmillan Education UK.

O'Regan, G. (2012). *A brief history of computing* (2nd ed.). Springer.

Rotella, E. J. (1981). The transformation of the American office: Changes in employment and technology. *The Journal of Economic History, 41*(1), 51–57. https://doi.org/10.1017/S0022050700042741

Sapkota, R., Roumeliotis, K. I., & Karkee, M. (2026). AI agents vs. agentic AI: A conceptual taxonomy, applications and challenges. *Information Fusion, 126*(Part B, February), 103599. https://doi.org/10.1016/j.inffus.2025.103599

van Dijk, J. (2020). *The digital divide*. Polity.

Vaswani, A., Shazeer, N., Parmar, N., Uszkoreit, J., Jones, L., Gomez, A. N., Kaiser, Ł., & Polosukhin, I. (2017). Attention is all you need. *Advances in Neural Information Processing Systems, 30*, 5998–6008.

CHAPTER 3

Affective Responses, Attitudes, and Use of AI

Abstract The use and adoption of AI are not simply questions of access. Research on technology acceptance has long shown that uptake depends on users' perceptions, attitudes, and expectations. AI elicits strong emotions because it is transforming working life faster than may feel comfortable for many workers. In this chapter, we present large-scale evidence on AI adoption among workers across 12 countries in six continents, examining not only whether workers use AI but how they use it and how their attitudes influence current uptake. We show and discuss meaningful cross-national differences in both AI use and trust toward AI and its developers. Moving beyond affective responses, the chapter also examines AI use as part of workers' identity processes and considers how concerns about AI-driven changes to work relate to adoption.

Keywords Attitude • Technology adoption • Trust • Human–computer interaction

> *Everything is becoming science fiction. [...] What the writers of modern science fiction invent today, you and I will do tomorrow. [...] The future is a better key to the present than the past.* J. G. Ballard (1971) in his nonfiction essay published in *Books and Bookmen.*

A. Oksanen, I. Savolainen, *AI Disruption at Work*, Palgrave Advances in Work and Organizational Psychology,
https://doi.org/10.1007/978-3-032-35207-1_3

Sentiments govern our world. Although AI has been hyped over the past years, it is worth remembering that a large part of our popular culture of the modern age has been filled with images of nonhuman intelligence, from *Frankenstein* (1818) to *Metropolis* (1927), and from *Blade Runner* (1982) to *Her* (2013). Science fiction has deeply influenced our culture and perceptions of AI, even before it was technically possible, as described by authors such as Isaac Asimov, Philip K. Dick, and William Gibson. Trust, hope, and doubt are projected on AI, and sentiments toward AI precede technical understanding of it. Even those who have first-hand experience with these tools often rely on and interpret AI through cultural images provided by fiction and popular imagination.

Responses and attitudes toward AI encompass more than simple notions of approval or rejection. People are not purely rational when making decisions but inherently feeling organisms that respond to stimuli, like new technologies, with both emotion and logic. Such responses can include expectations, anxiety, uncertainty, excitement, thrill, or sometimes indifference. In the context of work, AI typically evokes perceptions of both risk and opportunity. These expectations, feelings, and judgments influence how individuals choose to engage with AI, how organizations decide to handle its use, and how societies take on its broader implications. Today, AI use and diffusion touch more people than ever before. Its impact is mediated through the technical skills of individuals and meaning-making processes that guide resistance and adoption.

In this chapter, we bring together patterns of use, attitudes, and affective responses to AI. We analyze how AI tools are used globally across 12 countries based on *Self and Technology* project data. We show differences in the diffusion of generative AI (GenAI) use in 12 national contexts from six continents and then focus on factors explaining the use of AI tools. The analysis shows how AI use is influenced by attitudes and social psychological factors covering identity and self-efficacy. We then move on to sentiments and examine how trust and doubt coexist in public evaluations of AI. Drawing on longitudinal data from Finland, we explore changing perceptions of automation, job replacement, and AI's role in work. We conclude with a cross-national investigation of trust in AI and future expectations.

Adoption of AI Across Countries

The adoption of AI technologies at work has been remarkably fast, but research also indicates major differences across sectors and geographical areas. One study based on major U.S. firm-level 2018 data showed that early adoption of AI at work was limited to a small share of companies clustered in a handful of innovation hub cities (McElheran et al., 2024). These patterns indicate that AI diffusion in its early phase was constrained by significant organizational, technological, and infrastructural barriers. At the same time, AI development and deployment were largely driven by major organizations with the resources to invest in complementary assets, such as data, computing infrastructure, and organizational capabilities (Tyson & Zysman, 2022). We argue that many of these conditions have shifted in recent years, particularly with the emergence of widely accessible GenAI tools.

Our longitudinal surveys followed the same participants and their adoption of intelligent technologies. The *Self and Technology* study surveyed people about their use of new technologies, including GenAI tools such as ChatGPT, Gemini, and Copilot. Our survey asked about the use of the most common generative AI tools for text, image, or music creation. Questions on GenAI tools were also added to later waves as new tools emerged and were introduced to the public. Standard tools, such as ChatGPT, were the most used, but it was important to cover the different types of tools due to the variety of uses.

Figure 3.1 shows how the use of these tools has become more commonplace among Finnish, French, German, Irish, Italian, and Polish workers from 2023 to 2025. In our study, we followed the same individuals over time, and the figures show results for those whose occupational status was either employed, in a paid job, or an entrepreneur. In November 2023, approximately 1 year after the introduction of ChatGPT, the weekly use of GenAI tools was relatively uncommon in our samples, with some country differences. Our follow-up of the same individuals in these countries shows a rapid increase in 2024 and 2025. In autumn 2025, weekly GenAI use ranged from 25% in France to 35% in Ireland. Significant increases occurred, especially from 2024 to 2025, which is no surprise, considering the massive hype over AI in general.

Within the *Self and Technology* project, we had the opportunity to extend our data collection globally in 2024 with six additional countries (Australia, Brazil, Japan, Portugal, South Africa, and the United States).

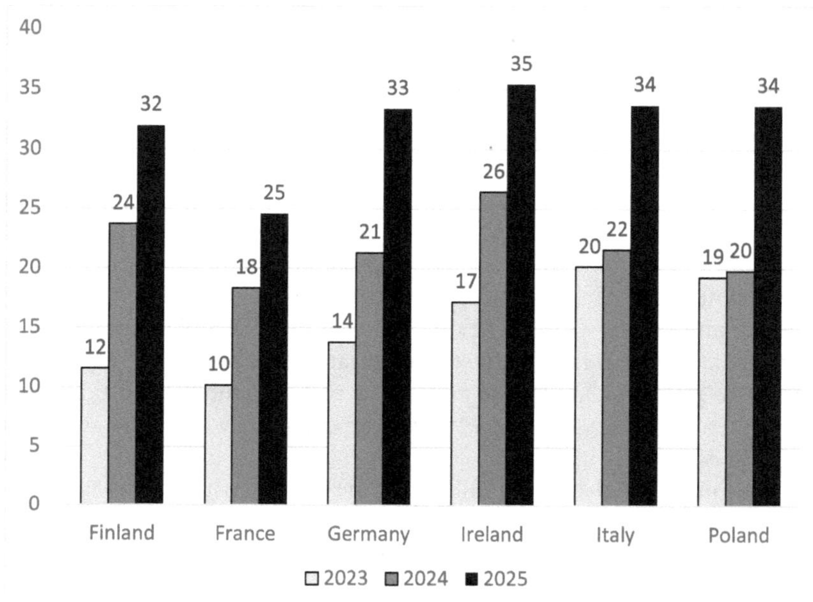

Fig. 3.1 Use of generative AI for work among workers in Finland, France, Germany, Ireland, Italy, and Poland, 2023–2025 (%). (Note: The same respondents participated in all three *SelfTech-EU-6* surveys (2023, 2024, and 2025). Results are based only on respondents whose main occupational status is a paid job or entrepreneur (or equivalent) and who report using GenAI tools at least occasionally. Analytical weights were applied.)

This cross-national approach allows us to examine how national contexts may condition AI uptake. Studies on the digital divide have previously emphasized disparities in access and rates of technology adoption (Lythreatis et al., 2022). More recently, OECD survey evidence extends this perspective by examining how AI is implemented, which workers interact with it, and for what purposes it is used. The findings suggest that these patterns vary by sector, firm size, worker characteristics, and type of application, with some differences also observed across national contexts (Lane et al., 2023).

Table 3.1 presents the share of employed respondents in our samples who reported using GenAI for work purposes, calculated only among respondents who had used generative AI at least occasionally. This

Table 3.1 Use of generative AI for work among employed generative AI users in 12 countries by education (%)

	No university education	*University education*	*All*
Australia	53	56	54
Brazil	69	78	73
Finland	38	58	47
France	21	49	35
Germany	27	49	38
Ireland	30	45	41
Italy	27	44	36
Japan	51	62	57
Poland	27	38	35
Portugal	47	54	50
South Africa	76	81	77
United States	46	59	52

Note: The table reports the percentage of GenAI use for work in each country. Results are based only on respondents whose main occupational status is a paid job or entrepreneur (or equivalent) and who report using GenAI tools at least occasionally. Data presented in the Table are based on the *Self and Technology* survey collected in Autumn 2024.

approach also improves cross-national comparability, given the differences in sample composition across countries. Table 3.1 shows differences in work-related GenAI use between respondents without a university degree and those with a university education, conditional on having used GenAI at least occasionally and being employed. Across all countries, respondents with a university education are more likely to report using GenAI for work, although the size of the educational gradient varies substantially. For example, the difference is very small in Australia (53% vs. 56%), while it is considerably larger in countries such as France (21% vs. 49%) and Finland (38% vs. 58%).

In Table 3.1, Brazil and South Africa stand out, with particularly high levels of work-related GenAI use across both educational groups. By contrast, several European countries display lower overall levels of AI work integration, especially among respondents without a university education, pointing to more institutionally mediated and role-specific patterns of adoption. We emphasize that our findings are based only on respondents with at least some experience with AI use. Nevertheless, we argue that the high levels of GenAI use observed in these countries cannot be explained by sampling effects alone.

In our samples, Brazil and South Africa could fit into the pattern of technological leapfrogging (i.e., skipping older versions of technologies and jumping directly into newer, more advanced solutions) in parts of the Global South (Cilliers, 2021; Khan et al., 2024). In the context of recent developments in AI, this involves fewer constraints by legislation or professional ecosystems. The United States, Japan, and the EU, for example, have heavier regulations, compliance, and intellectual property concerns. Lower organizational friction could, for example, involve faster uptake. GenAI essentially provides multifunctional help for work tasks. It is easily accessible and functions across languages. GenAI tools could also be integrated into informal workflows. As mobile technologies are already available in the Global South, GenAI could be used to solve many everyday problems, not only abstract ones. In addition, in Brazil and South Africa, there are lower expectations that either employers or the state will provide training, as formal employee training systems are currently limited or not in place (Sharma & Sharma, 2025). It is also possible that GenAI tools are used simply because they are a necessity. Under conditions of labor market precarity, using GenAI may become an implicit requirement, as workers are expected to keep up with technological changes.

Our longitudinal *WorkAI* survey provides a unique case of Finland and an interesting example of how AI has been adopted amid the AI disruption and what approaches workers have taken to cope with the change. Our data consist of a biannual follow-up survey, starting from autumn 2024 through autumn 2025. Figure 3.2 shows that daily use of AI tools for work increases only among those with a university degree (bachelor's to doctoral degrees) or a degree from universities of applied science (mostly bachelor's). The diffusion of use was rapid. At the same time, the data show that sectors characterized by a lower-educated workforce do not use AI for work despite its high potential for streamlining multiple tasks and providing quick access to information. The reality remains that this technology is everywhere, regardless of whether one is fixing a car or working in city gardens, reflecting the applications' manifold uses.

There are many potential reasons why this trend is observed in Finland. The first explanation is organizational: employees are encouraged to utilize only corporate-approved AI solutions. This is probably wise from a governance and risk-management perspective, but as workers are frequently warned about issues such as potential bias and hallucinations, among other factors, they might be reluctant to experiment and seek creative solutions on how to use AI on their own. Major corporations actively

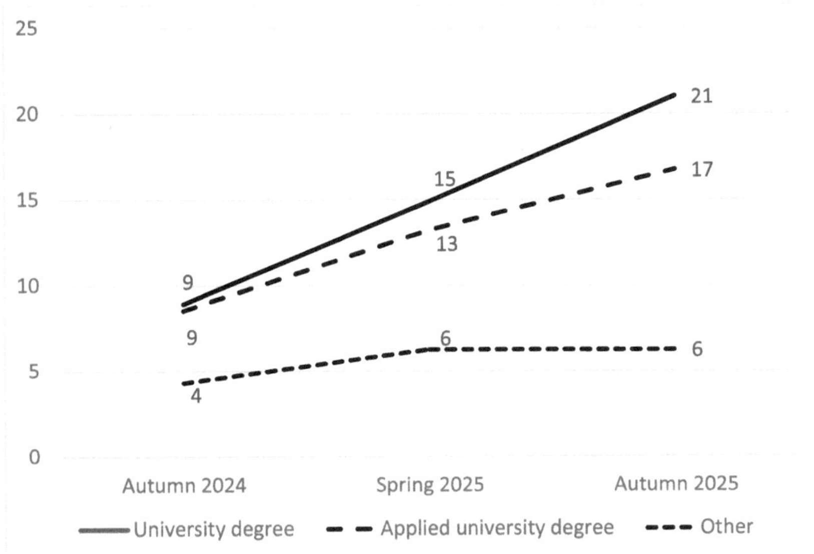

Fig. 3.2 Daily use of AI tools at work in Finland by university degree and time (%)

encourage AI use among their highly educated employees, whereas small to medium-sized enterprises (SME) have not necessarily kept up with the pace of these developments. This pattern is evidenced in recent OECD (2025) analyses. Furthermore, it is also possible that SMEs do not often have workers with the highest level of education. At least some small businesses are run by individuals with lower education, and although these firms could benefit substantially from AI, they may be less likely to adopt it or to encourage their employees to experiment with it due to, for instance, lower exposure and familiarity or unclear relevance for the tasks at hand.

The final interpretation of Fig. 3.2's results is less flattering. Despite Finland's seemingly good rankings globally on AI indices (e.g., position 15 on the Global AI Index; Tortoise Media, 2024), Fig. 3.2 shows that AI adoption appears uneven and concentrated among highly educated workers. The finding is alarming and refers to difficulties in AI adoption and scaling AI technologies to the work context. At the same time, these tools are very easy to use, but the benefits are only felt by those who use them and who are clever enough to apply them in novel ways. In this sense, AI-driven productivity and growth are a global, competitive process; as everyone is raising productivity, countries that fail to achieve broader adoption risk falling behind. Finland may represent a case in which strong digital foundations alone are insufficient when it comes to the era of AI disruption.

Attitudes, Identity, and Self-efficacy Explaining AI Use

Attitudes toward AI and any technology can be understood as relatively stable evaluations that individuals hold about a certain technology, including beliefs, feelings, and predispositions to engage with it (Kerschner & Ehlers, 2016; Stein et al., 2024). When it comes to AI emergence in today's workplace, these attitudes reflect how people assess AI in terms of usefulness, risks, desirability, and compatibility with their tasks and professional values (Savolainen et al., 2026). Importantly, attitudes are not simply cognitive judgments; they also involve emotional responses, such as enthusiasm and worry, which inherently influence how individuals relate to technological change. Attitudes are significant because they can impact at what rate and in what ways people engage with AI, and how smoothly it is incorporated into work practices. Even when AI tools are readily available, individuals differ in their appraisals and whether they choose to experiment with AI, integrate it into their everyday work processes, or avoid it altogether. These evaluations are also shaped by individual factors. Attitudes have been shown to relate to prior experience and digital skills, as well as demographic and psychological differences (e.g., age and openness to experience), which are likely to condition how AI is perceived and approached (Cai et al., 2017; de Freitas et al., 2023; Park & Woo, 2022). Therefore, attitudes are a key factor in initial adoption but also in sustained use, creative use, and resistance (Daly et al., 2025).

Research on technology use has traditionally relied on formal models to explain why individuals adopt or reject new technologies. One of the most influential frameworks is the Technology Acceptance Model (TAM; Davis et al., 1989) and its extensions (Venkatesh & Davis, 2000), which conceptualize adoption as an outcome of perceived usefulness and perceived ease of use. From this perspective, individuals are more likely to use technology when they believe it will improve their performance and when it is relatively easy to learn and operate. Models like TAM have provided valuable insight into patterns of technology uptake and use across a range of settings (King & He, 2006). Frameworks such as TAM can also be applied to current AI tools, given that human appraisals can be expected to be similar across technologies.

Building on this, the Unified Theory of Acceptance and Use of Technology (UTAUT; Venkatesh et al., 2003; Venkatesh, 2022) emphasizes that technology use is strongly determined by behavioral intention and that intention is influenced by several key factors: expectations about performance, perceptions of effort and usability, social pressures or norms, and the availability of supporting factors, such as training. UTAUT is particularly helpful in understanding the contextual factors of technology adoption, especially in situations where a work environment, for example, requires or encourages usage. A somewhat different lens to technology adoption is offered by the Diffusion of Innovation Theory (DOI; Rogers, 2003), which shifts attention away from individual acceptance and toward broader processes through which innovations spread. According to this theory, diffusion depends on the characteristics of innovation (e.g., perceived complexity), the attributes of adopters (e.g., prior experience and skills), and the surrounding social and organizational contexts (e.g., norms).

Traditional adoption models have remained relevant over the decades, in part because the dimensions through which they explain adoption can be applied across many contexts, primarily emphasizing human factors alongside some technology-related factors. However, their explanatory power also has limitations (Marangunić & Granić, 2015). In modern AI settings, these models may not be sufficient to capture the complexity of AI as a technology and the unique social and organizational dynamics that surround its use. Thus, while they offer important initial insights, these models may oversimplify the processes through which AI acceptance and adoption are formed.

Understanding AI use and acceptance also requires attention to how individuals perceive themselves and their capabilities in relation to technology. Identity and self-efficacy are central factors that provide important lenses for understanding how individuals respond to AI at work. Identity, referring to how people understand and define themselves in relation to their roles, skills, and personal values, shapes what individuals consider meaningful in their work and role, what competencies and skills they value, and how they interpret changes that impact their sense of expertise or status (Miscenko & Day, 2015).

When new technologies, such as AI, are introduced, individuals may perceive them either as aligning with or threatening these definitions of the self. Unlike prior new workplace technologies, AI has the ability to influence workers' roles more directly by assisting with core tasks, supporting decision-making, or in some cases, even replacing the worker's job or role altogether. At the same time, workers may see themselves as capable users of new technologies who can benefit from their digital skills and adapt to changing work environments, adjusting their self-perception and integrating AI as part of their professional identity (Perez et al., 2024) without necessarily experiencing negative consequences.

Self-efficacy, in contrast, refers to individuals' beliefs about their own ability to perform tasks successfully (Bandura, 1997). This includes a belief in mastering the use of new technologies, such as AI tools (Oksanen et al., 2026). When applied to AI, self-efficacy captures whether workers feel capable of learning, experimenting with, and effectively using AI systems. In everyday work, a sense of self-efficacy can significantly influence whether workers are willing or feel able to adapt to technological changes and continue using AI over time. High self-efficacy is often associated with a greater willingness to engage with new technologies, whereas low self-efficacy is associated with hesitation, anxiety, or avoidance (Hong, 2022; Montag et al., 2023).

Taken together, identity factors and self-efficacy both impact AI use and acceptance in ways that extend beyond traditional adoption models. Workers do not simply evaluate AI in terms of usefulness or ease of use but also assess whether they feel competent to adapt, what AI means for their work and roles, and who they are as professionals. For some, AI may reinforce a sense of capability and relevance, but for others, it may produce fears of deskilling, loss of control, or professional value. It is important to note that identity and self-efficacy are not purely individual traits. Rather, they are formed and reinforced through experience, interactions, training, and broader societal factors, such as in the case of AI, narratives about it. AI acceptance varies widely, even in contexts where access to AI is comparable, and recognizing these factors can help explain these differences.

Using the *Self and Technology* survey data across 12 countries, we tested how positive attitudes toward AI, AI learning readiness self-efficacy, and identity as a new technology user are associated with the likelihood of using GenAI at work. These logistic regression models (Table 3.2) support the view that attitudes alone are not sufficient for explaining AI use at work. Positive attitudes are sometimes associated with work use, whereas

Table 3.2 Predictors of AI use at work in 12 countries, based on logistic regression with average marginal effects

	AI positivity	*AI learning readiness self-efficacy*	*New tech user Identity*	*Model pseudo-R^2*
Australia	6.5%***	12.9%***	5.9%***	0.34
Brazil	4.6%*	12.3%***	6.7%***	0.26
Finland	5.4%*	6.9%**	4.0%*	0.22
France	8.1%**	5.7%*	1.3%	0.29
Germany	5.6%*	10.7%***	2.4%	0.27
Ireland	6.4%*	7.2%*	5.6%*	0.27
Italy	6.1%*	10.8%***	3.6%*	0.25
Japan	2.2%	12.9%*	13.7%***	0.35
Poland	3.1%	6.9%**	6.4%***	0.20
Portugal	7.3%***	9.4%***	8.2%***	0.19
South Africa	2.4%	9.6%***	7.5%***	0.30
United States	7.8%***	10.2%***	8.0%***	0.37

Note: Table shows average marginal effects from logistic regression, expressed as percentage points. Outcome variable is GenAI use for work (0 = no use, 1 = at least occasional use). All models were run separately for each country and involved only participants who worked. Continuous predictors were standardized (mean = 0, $SD = 1$). Gender, age, and education were adjusted. Statistical significance levels: *** $p < 0.001$, ** $p < 0.01$, * $p < 0.05$. Pseudo-R^2 indicates the relative model fit. The models are based on the *Self and Technology* survey data from Autumn 2024.

AI learning readiness self-efficacy and new technology user identity emerge as more consistent predictors. In other words, workers who feel capable of learning and using AI, and who see themselves as the type of person who adopts and benefits from new technologies are more likely to report using GenAI in their work. Specifically, a one standard deviation increase in AI learning readiness self-efficacy is associated with an approximately 10-percentage-point higher probability of using GenAI for work. The magnitude of this association varies across countries, reaching its highest level in Australia and Japan (12.9%). Technological identity is also positively associated with AI use, corresponding to a higher probability of work-related AI use across most countries. Positive attitudes toward AI show a weaker but still meaningful association. The increase ranged from 2.2% in Japan (not statistically significant) to 7.8% in the United States.

Between Trust and Doubt

In *Contingencies of Reinforcement* (1969), American psychologist B. F. Skinner famously observed that "the real problem is not whether machines think but whether men do" (p. 265). Although this remark was expressed well before today's AI and technological advancements, its relevance echoes today. Trust plays a central role in shaping how individuals engage with technology. It can be understood as the willingness to rely on a system under conditions of uncertainty, including expectations about the system's competence, reliability, and its alignment with the user's intentions (Saßmannshausen et al., 2023). In today's context, AI systems increasingly participate in decision-making by providing recommendations, predictions, and content, thus transforming work processes, evaluations, and professional judgment. The central challenge, therefore, is not only whether these systems can be trusted but also how humans maintain judgment, reflection, and responsibility in their use. Skinner's concern reflects a warning that people may stop thinking critically, surrendering judgment, responsibility, and agency to systems they treat as authoritative. This raises a key question for today's users: When is trust appropriate, and when is doubt necessary?

Trust in technology is not a uniform condition but can take different forms, depending on how users relate to a system or its outputs and content. Research on human–technology interaction has shown that appraisals of trust can be distinguished between overtrust, undertrust, and accurate assessment, or calibrated trust (de Visser et al., 2020; Lucas et al., 2024; Ullrich et al., 2021). Overtrust occurs when individuals rely too readily on a system, accepting the outputs it produces without critically evaluating them and overlooking judgment, even when errors occur or are apparent. Undertrust, on the other hand, reflects high skepticism, where users disregard or avoid technologies that would otherwise be useful or have demonstrated reliability. Both of these trust types represent different ends of the spectrum of trust and can be problematic. Overtrust may lead to errors or overreliance on technology, whereas undertrust is related to missed opportunities and lower productivity.

Between these two ends lies calibrated trust, which refers to an appropriate balance between a user's level of trust and a system's actual trustworthiness in terms of capabilities and limitations. Applied to AI, calibrated trust allows individuals to rely on AI where it performs well, given that the user remains attentive and critical, and willing to intervene when necessary. Achieving such balanced trust, however, can be challenging.

Prior research suggests that the drivers of trust in AI can be grouped into three broad categories: factors related to the human user, factors related to the AI system itself, and contextual features of the interaction between the two (Kaplan et al., 2021). Among system-related factors, performance and reliability are consistently related to trust. If an AI system appears accurate and dependable, users are more likely to trust it. However, AI systems are often invisible or operate opaquely, generate random and sometimes inconsistent outputs, and change over time, making it difficult to evaluate when trust is warranted. Thus, trust in AI tends to be dynamic and situational rather than stable (Glikson & Woolley, 2020; Oksanen & Savolainen, 2025). Human-related factors matter as well. For example, users' competence and confidence, both in their own expertise and ability to work with AI, can positively influence trust in AI, as individuals who feel capable have a better position in evaluating outputs and deciding when trust is appropriate (Kaplan et al., 2021).

Concerns about job loss and displacement are among the most common worries surrounding AI. This is understandable, as AI systems increasingly perform tasks that were previously done and considered to continue to be done exclusively by humans, such as writing, decision-making, or creative work. Workers today may perceive AI both as a tool and as a potential competitor and threat (Savela et al., 2024). These concerns are accompanied and influenced by uncertainty about the direction and pace of technological development and change and the role of organizations in renewing their work models. We examined the technology-related worries of Finnish workers, utilizing the 14-time-point longitudinal *WorkSome* survey data collected between 2019 and 2025. Given this timeframe, we have been able to follow workers over major societal disruptions, such as the COVID-19 pandemic and the most recent AI emergence. The data show that concerns over robots replacing people's jobs declined between 2019 and 2022, after which they started to show a new upward trend. Fears of new technologies putting one's work at risk remained relatively steady but started to rise slightly toward the end of 2025. The worry over AI replacing human work demonstrated a rapid increase in autumn 2022 and has continued to increase since (Fig. 3.3). However, it should be noted that fears of displacement do not necessarily equate to the rejection of technology by workers; rather, it is an added element that comes

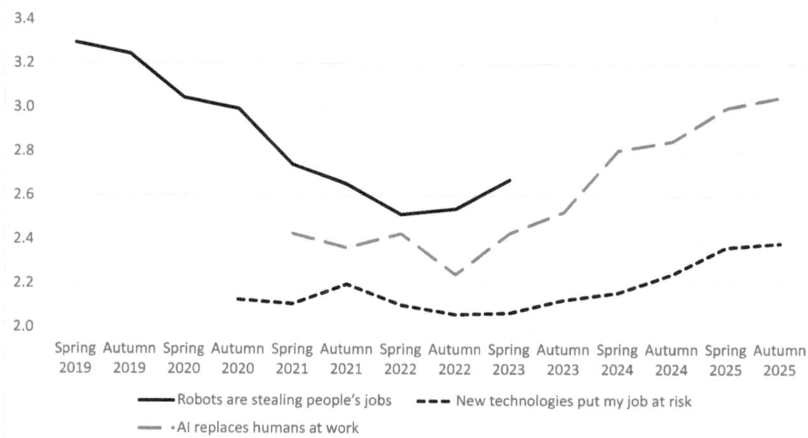

Fig. 3.3 Worries about new technologies replacing humans in Finland in 2019–2025. (Note: The figure is based on the 14-time-point longitudinal *WorkSome* survey data collected biannually. The results are on a scale from 1 (*strongly disagree*) to 7 (*strongly agree*).)

with AI disruption and naturally leads to assessments of risk in the context of salient job insecurity or uneven organizational support.

Many workers expressed positive appraisals of AI and recognized its potential benefits alongside perceived risks. The cross-national *SelfTech-EU-6* data indicate relatively high levels of positive attitudes toward AI across the six countries, although some changes can be observed over the past 4 years (Fig. 3.4). In Germany, Italy, and Poland, positive attitudes have generally increased, while Finland shows a more pronounced downward trend, with declines also observed in France and Ireland. These patterns suggest that optimism about AI remains widespread, but national contexts with potential differences in workplace conditions and public discourse influence how positive attitudes have developed over time.

Positive expectations of AI are commonly evident where AI is perceived as augmenting rather than replacing human capabilities and positions (Savolainen et al., 2026). For many workers, AI represents new opportunities in working life, whether enhancing their current tasks, enhancing skills, increasing productivity, or opening whole new professions. More

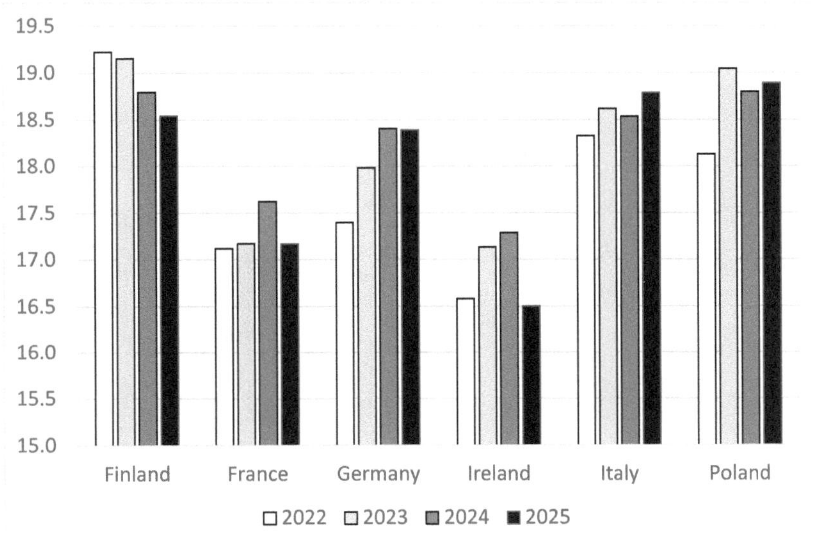

Fig. 3.4 Positive attitude toward AI across six European countries in 2022–2025. (Note: The figure is based on the *SelfTech-EU-6* longitudinal data. Dependent variable is positive AI attitude (range 4–28, see Appendix). The results here are from participants who participated in all four survey waves. Analytical weights were used. The scale of positive AI attitude ranged from 4 (*very low*) to 28 (*very high*).)

positive appraisals are often associated with prior experience with AI or digital technologies, openness, and confidence in one's ability to use AI as well as supporting organizational environments that encourage experimentation and use rather than imposing restrictive rules (Daly et al., 2025; Park & Woo, 2022; Schepman & Rodway, 2023). In addition, when workers have appropriate trust in AI systems, they are more likely to integrate them into everyday tasks (Cvetkovic et al., 2026). Without at least a baseline level of trust, even highly sophisticated tools may remain underused.

A related but distinct issue around trust in the AI landscape is trust in the organizations that design, develop, and create new AI systems for users. Trust, therefore, extends beyond an individual's interactions with AI to include those actors who make AI possible for everyday users. In the *SelfTech-EU-6* longitudinal survey, we investigated individuals' trust in

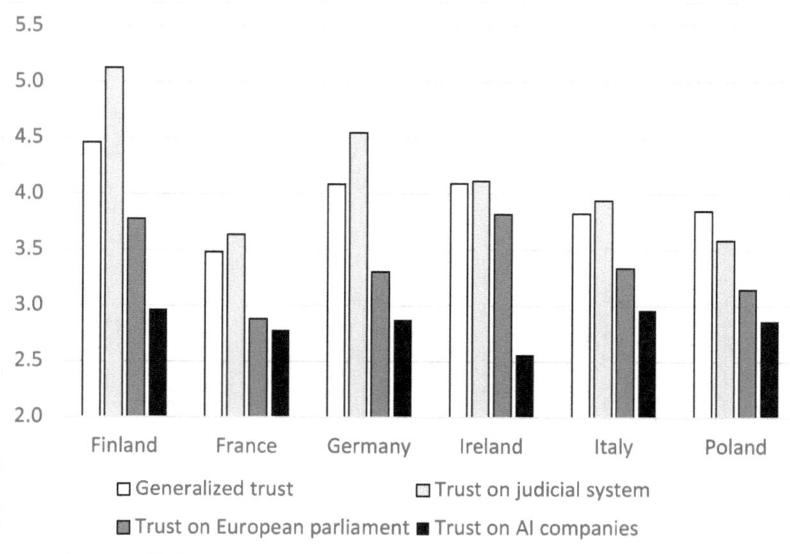

Fig. 3.5 Generalized trust, institutional trust, and trust in companies developing AI across six European countries in autumn 2025. (Note: The figure is based on *SelfTech-EU-6* data from autumn 2025. Trust was measured on a scale from 1 (*I do not trust at all*) to 7 (*I trust completely*). Analytical weights were used.)

companies developing AI as well as their broader judgments about the judicial system (in their respective country), trust in the European Parliament, and their generalized trust. This ties the question of trusting AI into corporate responsibility and governance, which are relevant factors in large-scale societal change. The most recent data measured in the autumn of 2025 (Fig. 3.5) show that generalized trust was moderate across the six countries (averaging between 3.5 and 4.5 on a scale from 1 to 7). Trust in judicial systems was slightly higher than generalized trust in each country except for Poland, with the highest level of trust in judicial systems in Finland followed by Germany. France demonstrated the lowest trust in judicial systems. Trust in the European Parliament was modest, with Ireland and Finland showing the highest trust (3.8) and France showing the lowest (2.9).

The survey respondents' trust in companies developing AI was relatively low. The highest trust in companies was measured in Finland and Italy (averaging 3 on the 1–7 scale) and lowest in Ireland (with an average of 2.6). These results reveal interesting patterns. Although trust in companies developing AI is low among Europeans in the sample, AI use remains widespread. This suggests that users' trust in AI is separate from the company that created it. This has been demonstrated before in people's technology use, where they use a platform (e.g., social media) without trusting the platform provider or developer (Cvetkovic et al., 2026). In the case of AI and the context of work, it is likely that workers rely on institutional guidelines and safeguards and their own judgment when deciding how to engage with AI. It is also possible that users' trust is conditional, and they use it when it appears useful and reliable.

The above-mentioned interpretation is supported by the further analysis of our data, which showed that daily use of AI at work and perceived competence in AI predicted future optimism, measured with the statement, "Much of society will benefit from a future full of Artificial Intelligence" (Fig. 3.6). In the figure, we can see that as perceived AI

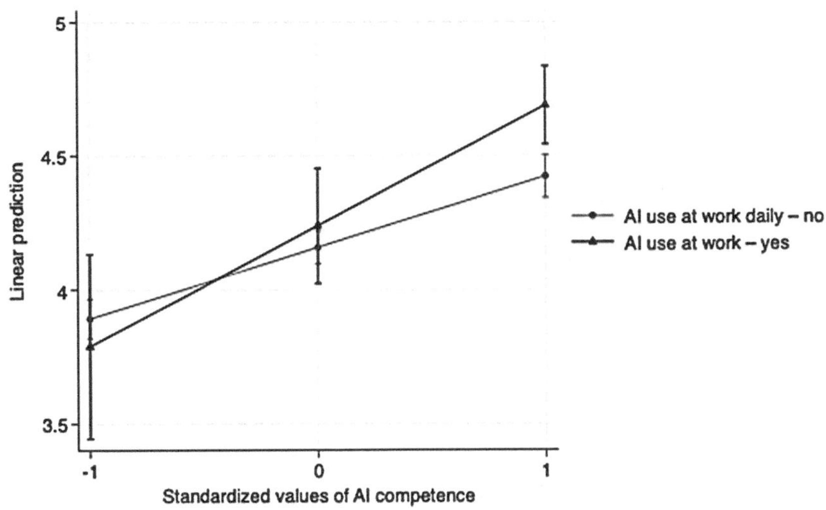

Fig. 3.6 AI future optimism in Finland (predictive margins with 95% confidence intervals). (Note: The figure is based on the *WorkAI* longitudinal data from Finland (3 waves in 2024–2025). The figure shows AI future optimism measured with the statement, "Much of society will benefit from a future full of Artificial Intelligence" with a response scale from 1 (*strongly disagree*) to 7 (*strongly agree*). This is based on random-effects GLS regression on 1385 Finnish workers taking part in all three waves from 2024 to 2025.)

competence increases, so does future optimism. The association between AI competence and future optimism is stronger among those who utilize AI at work on a daily basis.

Conclusion: The Social Psychology of AI Adoption

New innovations always elicit emotional and cognitive responses and inevitably influence how we perceive, interpret, and respond to technological change. AI is no exception. As this chapter has shown, workers' responses to AI are characterized by a complex interplay of attitudes, affective reactions, trust, and worry. In that sense, AI entering our lives and workplaces is proving to be as much a social and psychological as a technical process.

Over the decades, research on attitudes has provided insight into technology acceptance and adoption. Such frameworks provide a valuable understanding of how people perceive and respond to new technologies, yet even positive attitudes do not consistently translate into use and adoption. Something has been missing from the equation, especially as the technologies themselves evolve beyond the assumptions of traditional models explaining usage. A central insight of this chapter is to identify part of that missing piece. Rather than viewing AI use as merely a choice made based on rational reasoning or an immediate emotional response, there are deeper factors that are more meaningful to individuals and workers. Self-efficacy and identity have emerged as more robust predictors of AI use than attitudes, indicating that whether individuals feel capable of engaging with AI and whether doing so aligns with their sense of who they are as workers can either undermine or support AI use. Thus, AI's current impact on work is not determined solely by what technologies can do but by how people make sense of them. AI change is not experienced only as an external force; it is experienced at the individual level through confidence, competence, and professional self-understanding.

The fact that AI use is spreading across workplaces at a high rate suggests that, alongside concerns, many workers also perceive the real benefits of these tools. Research already points to AI's potential in supporting efficiency and productivity, and adding balance and meaning to work, while workers maintain their agency and competence (Savolainen et al., 2026). Going forward, understanding AI's role in working life requires moving beyond major narratives of resistance versus acceptance and toward a more nuanced investigation of how people continue to negotiate the existing uncertainties and how they maintain their agency and make sense of change. Social psychological research offers tools for understanding processes such as identity negotiation, meaning making, and perceived control, helping to explain whether workers use AI and how they experience it and incorporate it into their everyday lives. In the next chapters, we build on these foundations and focus more on professional identity and self-efficacy.

References

Ballard, J. G. (1971). Fictions of every kind. *Books and Bookmen*. https://www.jgballard.ca/non_fiction/jgb_fictions.html

Bandura, A. (1997). *Self-efficacy: The exercise of control*. W. H. Freeman and Company.

Cai, Z., Fan, X., & Du, J. (2017). Gender and attitudes toward technology use: A meta-analysis. *Computers & Education, 105*, 1–13. https://doi.org/10.1016/j.compedu.2016.11.003

Cilliers, J. (2021). Technological innovation and the power of Leapfrogging. In J. Cilliers (Ed.), *The future of Africa* (pp. 253–284). Palgrave Macmillan. https://doi.org/10.1007/978-3-030-46590-2_10

Cvetkovic, A., Savolainen, I., Celuch, M., Heiskari, M., Soares Ruokosuo, E., Arriaga, P., Koike, M., & Oksanen, A. (2026). User trust in AI and major tech companies in twelve countries. *Behaviour & Information Technology*, 1–17. https://doi.org/10.1080/0144929X.2026.2619648

Daly, S. J., Wiewiora, A., & Hearn, G. (2025). Shifting attitudes and trust in AI: Influences on organizational AI adoption. *Technological Forecasting and Social Change, 215*, 124108. https://doi.org/10.1016/j.techfore.2025.124108

Davis, F. D., Bagozzi, R. P., & Warshaw, P. R. (1989). User acceptance of computer technology: A comparison of two theoretical models. *Management Science, 35*(8), 982–1003. https://doi.org/10.1287/mnsc.35.8.982

de Freitas, J., Agarwal, S., Schmitt, B., & Haslam, N. (2023). Psychological factors underlying attitudes toward AI tools. *Nature Human Behaviour, 7*(11), 1845–1854. https://doi.org/10.1038/s41562-023-01734-2

de Visser, E. J., Peeters, M. M., Jung, M. F., Kohn, S., Shaw, T. H., Pak, R., & Neerincx, M. A. (2020). Towards a theory of longitudinal trust calibration in human–robot teams. *International Journal of Social Robotics, 12*(2), 459–478. https://doi.org/10.1007/s12369-019-00596-x

Glikson, E., & Woolley, A. W. (2020). Human trust in artificial intelligence: Review of empirical research. *Academy of Management Annals, 14*(2), 627–660. https://doi.org/10.5465/annals.2018.0057

Hong, J. W. (2022). I was born to love AI: The influence of social status on AI self-efficacy and intentions to use AI. *International Journal of Communication, 16*, 172–191.

Kaplan, A. D., Kessler, T. T., Brill, J. C., & Hancock, P. A. (2021). Trust in artificial intelligence: Meta-analytic findings. *Human Factors: The Journal of the Human Factors and Ergonomics Society, 65*(2), 337–359. https://doi.org/10.1177/00187208211013988

Kerschner, C., & Ehlers, M. H. (2016). A framework of attitudes towards technology in theory and practice. *Ecological Economics, 126*, 139–151. https://doi.org/10.1016/j.ecolecon.2016.02.010

Khan, M. S., Umer, H., & Faruqe, F. (2024). Artificial intelligence for low income countries. *Humanities and Social Sciences Communications, 11*(1), 1–13. https://doi.org/10.1057/s41599-024-03947-w

King, W. R., & He, J. (2006). A meta-analysis of the technology acceptance model. *Information & Management, 43*(6), 740–755. https://doi.org/10.1016/j.im.2006.05.003

Lane, M., Williams, M., & Broecke, S. (2023). The impact of AI on the workplace: Main findings from the OECD AI surveys of employers and workers. *OECD Social, Employment and Migration Working Papers*, No. 288. OECD Publishing. https://doi.org/10.1787/ea0a0fe1-en.

Lucas, G. M., Becerik-Gerber, B., & Roll, S. C. (2024). Calibrating workers' trust in intelligent automated systems. *Patterns, 5*(9), 101045. https://doi.org/10.1016/j.patter.2024.101045

Lythreatis, S., Singh, S. K., & El-Kassar, A. N. (2022). The digital divide: A review and future research agenda. *Technological Forecasting and Social Change, 175*, 121359. https://doi.org/10.1016/j.techfore.2021.121359

Marangunić, N., & Granić, A. (2015). Technology acceptance model: A literature review from 1986 to 2013. *Universal Access in the Information Society, 14*(1), 81–95. https://doi.org/10.1007/s10209-014-0348-1

McElheran, K., Li, J. F., Brynjolfsson, E., Kroff, Z., Dinlersoz, E., Foster, L., & Zolas, N. (2024). AI adoption in America: Who, what, and where. *Journal of Economics & Management Strategy, 33*(2), 375–415. https://doi.org/10.1111/jems.12576

Miscenko, D., & Day, D. V. (2015). Identity and identification at work. *Organizational Psychology Review, 6*(3), 215–247. https://doi.org/10.1177/2041386615584009

Montag, C., Kraus, J., Baumann, M., & Rozgonjuk, D. (2023). The propensity to trust in (automated) technology mediates the links between technology self-efficacy and fear and acceptance of artificial intelligence. *Computers in Human Behavior Reports, 11*, 100315. https://doi.org/10.1016/j.chbr.2023.100315

OECD. (2025). *AI adoption by small and medium-sized enterprises. OECD discussion paper for the G7*. OECD Publishing. https://doi.org/10.1787/426399c1-en

Oksanen, A., Osma, T., Heiskari, M., Cvetkovic, A., Soares Ruokosuo, E., Koike, M., Arriaga, P., & Savolainen, I. (2026). Mapping AI learning readiness self-efficacy worldwide: Scale validation and cross-continental patterns. *Computers in Human Behavior: Artificial Humans, 7*, 100251. https://doi.org/10.1016/j.chbah.2026.100251

Oksanen, A., & Savolainen, I. (2025). Trust in emerging technologies and artificial intelligence. In K. J. Rotenberg, S. Petrocchi, A. Levante, & F. Lecciso (Eds.), *The handbook of trust and social psychology* (pp. 184–205). Edward Elgar Publishing Limited. https://doi.org/10.4337/9781803929415.00023

Park, J., & Woo, S. E. (2022). Who likes artificial intelligence? Personality predictors of attitudes toward artificial intelligence. *The Journal of Psychology, 156*(1), 68–94. https://doi.org/10.1080/00223980.2021.2012109

Perez, F., Conway, N., Peterson, J., & Roques, O. (2024). Me, my work and AI: How radiologists craft their work and identity. *Journal of Vocational Behavior, 155*, 104042. https://doi.org/10.1016/j.jvb.2024.104042

Rogers, E. M. (2003). *Diffusion of innovations* (5th ed.). Free Press.

Saßmannshausen, T., Burggräf, P., Hassenzahl, M., & Wagner, J. (2023). Human trust in otherware – a systematic literature review bringing all antecedents together. *Ergonomics, 66*(7), 976–998. https://doi.org/10.1080/00140139.2022.2120634

Savela, N., Garcia, D., Pellert, M., & Oksanen, A. (2024). Emotional talk about robotic technologies on Reddit: Sentiment analysis of life domains, motives, and temporal themes. *New Media & Society, 26*(2), 757–781. https://doi.org/10.1177/14614448211067259

Savolainen, I., Ylinen, L., Grönroos, R., & Oksanen, A. (2026). AI transformation in working life: A systematic review of usage and attitudes towards AI among workers. *Digital Business, 6*(1), 100162. https://doi.org/10.1016/j.digbus.2025.100162

Schepman, A., & Rodway, P. (2023). The general attitudes towards artificial intelligence scale (GAAIS): Confirmatory validation and associations with personality, corporate distrust, and general trust. *International Journal of Human–Computer Interaction, 39*(13), 2724–2741. https://doi.org/10.1080/10447318.2022.2085400

Sharma, A. K., & Sharma, R. (2025). Governance in the age of artificial intelligence: A comparative analysis of policy framework in BRICS nations. *AI Magazine, 46*(2), e70010. https://doi.org/10.1002/aaai.70010

Skinner, B. F. (1969). *Contingencies of reinforcement: A theoretical analysis.* Prentice Hall.

Stein, J. P., Messingschlager, T., Gnambs, T., Hutmacher, F., & Appel, M. (2024). Attitudes towards AI: Measurement and associations with personality. *Scientific Reports, 14*(1), 2909. https://doi.org/10.1038/s41598-024-53335-2

Tortoise Media. (2024). The Global AI Index ranking. https://www.tortoisemedia.com/data/global-ai#rankings

Tyson, L. D., & Zysman, J. (2022). Automation, AI & work. *Daedalus, 151*(2), 256–271. https://doi.org/10.1162/daed_a_01914

Ullrich, D., Butz, A., & Diefenbach, S. (2021). The development of overtrust: An empirical simulation and psychological analysis in the context of human–robot interaction. *Frontiers in Robotics and AI, 8*, 554578. https://doi.org/10.3389/frobt.2021.554578

Venkatesh, V. (2022). Adoption and use of AI tools: A research agenda grounded in UTAUT. *Annals of Operations Research, 308*(1), 641–652. https://doi.org/10.1007/s10479-020-03918-9

Venkatesh, V., & Davis, F. D. (2000). A theoretical extension of the technology acceptance model: Four longitudinal field studies. *Management Science, 46*(2), 186–204. https://doi.org/10.1287/mnsc.46.2.186.11926

Venkatesh, V., Morris, M. G., Davis, G. B., & Davis, F. D. (2003). User acceptance of information technology: Toward a unified view. *MIS Quarterly, 27*(3), 425–478. https://doi.org/10.2307/30036540

CHAPTER 4

Professional Identity in Transition

Abstract Professional identity refers to a developing sense of "who I am" at work. It is molded by everyday experiences, relationships, and personal values. This sense of self is continuously revised over time as workers aim to preserve their professional meaning, protect what they care about, and adapt to new expectations. This chapter examines work as a source of identity and investigates how the growing use of AI in workplaces can prompt identity changes or threats for workers. Identity threats may emerge in multiple forms, partly because AI systems differ so widely and partly because people's roles, resources, and meanings attached to work also vary. Such threats can be experienced as challenges to competence, autonomy, and perceived worth. This chapter presents findings on AI-related stressors that can intensify these experiences and highlights factors that may buffer strain, support coping, and help workers maintain a coherent sense of professional identity amid disruption. We clarify when and by whom AI is more likely experienced as a tool that extends expertise versus a potential threat to professional identity.

Keywords Professional identity • Stress • Coping • Well-being • Artificial intelligence

A. Oksanen, I. Savolainen, *AI Disruption at Work*, Palgrave Advances in Work and Organizational Psychology,
https://doi.org/10.1007/978-3-032-35207-1_4

AI profoundly changes how people perceive their work. This aspect of AI touches on the social psychological foundations of work. Professional expertise requires years of practice and training, and work often becomes part of how people understand themselves. In some fields, experts realized early on that AI could do things that were precisely their expertise. In the cultural and creative industries, one of the most well-known cases involves Hollywood screenwriters. In 2023, more than 11,000 members of the Writers Guild of America went on strike in one of the largest Hollywood labor actions in more than a decade, due to contract disagreements and to help ensure that AI tools could not be used to replace or undermine human writing. With streaming services and production companies needing writers less often and hiring fewer writers when needed, screenwriters were essentially becoming gig workers with smaller compensation and a loss of working conditions (Guardian, 2023). AI undoubtedly jeopardized their work, voices, and crafts. This raised existential questions about what it means to be a screenwriter and storyteller in an age in which everything could be generated and regenerated instantly. Most importantly, the strikes and debates that continued afterward were mostly not about wages but about professional identity.

The example of Hollywood screenwriters underlines the centrality of identities in AI disruption at work. Individuals often describe themselves in terms of what they do for a living. Through work, people develop a sense of purpose, competence, belonging, and professional identity (Chreim et al., 2007). These are also key elements in intrinsic motivation. When work changes, it is not only tasks or skills that are affected but also how workers see themselves and their place in the world of work. As discussed in earlier chapters, AI is unique when compared to other new technologies. Its broad range of applications is not merely used by workers, but its different applications and features can also extend or augment people or even do their work for them. For some workers, AI may reinforce a sense of capability and competence, but for others, it may induce uncertainty, particularly regarding one's relevance and professional worth. Investigating professional identity amid transition allows us to look beyond questions of adoption and gain a deeper understanding of how workers respond to AI change.

This chapter addresses this dimension of AI disruption that has so far received limited attention: the role of the self in shaping how technological change is experienced and managed at work. We examine how workers across different sectors and roles experience AI in relation to their professional identities. The current emergence of AI poses significant stress to worker identity. This particularly involves fields that have previously been dominated only by human work. We draw evidence from *WorkAI* surveys conducted in Finland that examine how professionals experience and negotiate their identities during periods of technological change. Additionally, we consider the stressors associated with this transformation and the coping strategies individuals employ in response.

Work as a Source of Identity

How people perceive themselves is central to well-being and behavior. In social psychology, the self comprises three dimensions: self-concept (i.e., how we perceive ourselves), public self (i.e., how we connect with others socially), and agent self (i.e., how we act and make choices) (Baumeister, 2022; Baumeister & Bushman, 2020). Self-concept could also be called self-knowledge, and it involves self-awareness, self-esteem, and information about the self and refers to how we perceive and understand ourselves. The public self refers to our interpersonal self and involves social roles, social identities, and the way we present ourselves in social situations. The agent self is the executive part of the self and involves our decisions, self-control, and control over other people and things. This social psychological notion of the self (Baumeister, 2022) is consistent with developmental and life-course perspectives (e.g., Crocetti et al., 2023; Schwartz, 2001).

Self-concept, public self, and agent self overlap and are all deeply grounded in various social and cultural settings and relationships with others. In social and cultural psychology, a considerable amount of research has been conducted to determine the ways in which culture affects the self. One important distinction is the difference between those cultures that consider the self independent and those that consider the self interdependent (Kitayama et al., 1997; Markus & Kitayama, 2010). This is directly related to cultural variation in self-expression values (Inglehart & Welzel, 2005) and individualism (Triandis, 2018). The way we perceive ourselves in relation to others is likely to have an impact on how we use technologies to communicate with others, make social comparisons, and verify our self-concept and identities.

Self-concept is related to the concept of identity. The term identity derives from the Latin word "idem," meaning "the same," and refers to the relatively coherent and stable understanding individuals have of themselves (Jenkins, 2014). People narrate themselves for who they are and express these views publicly. In social psychological theory, identity is often analytically distinguished into personal and social dimensions (Harré, 1983). Personal identity (the "I") refers to the unique distinctiveness of a person compared to other people. Social identities are public group–based identities, which have been extensively discussed in studies conducted within the social identity approach (Brown, 2020). This approach emphasizes how identification with social groups, including occupational and organizational groups, modifies self-definition and behavior (Ashforth & Mael, 1989; Haslam, 2012). Personal and social identities are not separate or competing dimensions of the self. Rather, they are intertwined. They jointly affect how individuals perceive themselves in certain places and times, considering continuity and change over time.

Research on work identity has traditionally drawn on identity theory, which conceptualizes identity as tied to work roles and relatively stable over time (Miscenko & Day, 2016). From this perspective, work identity can be understood as consisting of attributes that are closely associated with one's role, such as title, tasks, and responsibilities. Importantly, work identity is constructed from multiple sources. The organizations in which individuals are employed are one source, as they offer said roles, norms, and feedback systems that influence how workers understand themselves in the workplace. In addition, research has shown that many individuals increasingly ground their identities in occupational membership, which is becoming more salient as careers become more mobile and boundaries between jobs and organizations are less clear (Walsh & Gordon, 2008). A central mechanism in work identity is self-verification; the process through which workers confirm their professional identities. It is typically established by carrying out behaviors that are consistent with the identity and by receiving affirmation from peers. Workers, therefore, actively seek roles and environments that allow them to carry out such acts and express and validate identity meanings. When workers are unable to verify the core aspects of their professional identities, they may experience negative effects, such as strain and emotional exhaustion (Hall et al., 2015; Yang & Zhang, 2023).

As already noted in Chap. 3, identity plays a role in technology use. People, as social animals, group together and are influenced by others around them, forming social identities very easily. These in-group identifications are likely to affect how technologies are perceived and adopted (Heiskari et al., 2025; Savela et al., 2021). Furthermore, in an increasingly technology-mediated world, people are obsessed with mirroring themselves via social media (Savolainen et al., 2025). This example shows how technologies change the public validation of ourselves. New technologies also affect the more private sides of the self—or personal identity—and offer multiple ways for people to collect feedback and data and reflect on how they are doing, often in comparison to others. Navigating today's digital context is relatively new to people, and technology has profoundly shifted how we undertake these self-evaluations. Individuals no longer have to rely on direct social interaction and experiences but can utilize large amounts of data, typically driven by algorithms, to make judgments and apply different beliefs and ideas to the self. As a result, questions such as "who I am" are often mediated by technology.

Similar processes also affect professional settings. When technologies are integrated into workflows, they are bound to influence what is considered valuable and distinctive human work. Over time, this will also change how people assess and feel about themselves in their abilities and as professionals—and how they perceive their position in relation to others. AI intensifies these dynamics at a rate that we have not witnessed before. It participates directly in activities that have so far been defined through professional expertise that is typically achieved after years of studying, gaining experience, and doing the work. Having a technology such as AI conduct, for instance, your analyses faster and more accurately or write a script with an unexpected twist is likely to evoke a response in a worker and prompt them to renegotiate their professional identity, both personally and in comparison to colleagues, whose responses may differ.

In social psychology, identity at work is an ongoing and evolving topic. Breakwell's (1986) *Coping with Threatened Identities* covers a topic that is still relevant today. It analyzes how people respond to situations in which their selves are challenged or destabilized. For Breakwell (1986), identity involves a sense of continuity, which means being the same person over time. Identity or, in this case, personal identity also involves the distinctiveness of being unique from others. This is to say that despite having our social or group identities, for example, as members of a certain nationality or profession, our personal identities often involve what makes us different from others. An essential part of this personal identity is self-esteem or self-worth. Although identities may appear coherent and continuous at a particular time and place, identities are not static; they change over time and can be threatened internally and externally. External events might threaten the continuity or value of the work role or status. Changes could cause inconsistencies that require people to adjust their self-definitions internally. In addition, identities can be threatened socially, as they need to be socially recognized and validated.

Recent research has begun to conceptualize AI identity threat as the perception that AI technologies potentially undermine, destabilize, or devalue workers' established self-beliefs and professional identities (Craig et al., 2019; Jussupow et al., 2022; Mirbabaie et al., 2022). More generally, identity threat refers to experiences that have the ability to harm the meaning or value of an identity that is perceived to be important and relatively stable. Identity threats can be anticipated if they emerge from, for example, potential cues to job loss or changes to existing roles. Applied to AI, identity threats arise when intelligent systems take on tasks that previously relied on the worker's defined expertise. Thus, AI's integration puts into question the stability of workers' roles and their distinctive contributions. These processes are inherently social and psychological. Identity threat is influenced by how workers interpret and anticipate its impact through comparison, feedback, and expectations about one's future of work. When faced with AI, workers actively appraise it and evaluate whether it affirms or undermines their sense of professional value and competence. These appraisals inform whether AI is approached as an opportunity or a threat.

We investigated Finnish workers' identity threats across three dimensions—worth, competence, and authenticity—using the *WorkAI* longitudinal survey data. Examining changes over a year, we found that the background factors explaining the three AI identity threat dimensions were consistent, as shown in Table 4.1. The perception of AI-based identity threats was lower among older workers and those with at least a bachelor's degree. Entrepreneurs reported significantly lower AI identity threats, but supervisors reported higher perceptions of threats. This suggests that AI might challenge those in positions of authority and responsibility. Occupational differences were included in the models but did not show significant differences aside from those in health and care, who generally reported a lower perception of threats. It is worth noting that daily AI use was unrelated to AI identity threats, while organizational AI adoption showed only a small positive association with competence threat.

Our findings indicate that AI identity threat is not an inevitable outcome of technological change but a possible experience that is dependent

Table 4.1 Longitudinal models explaining AI identity threat in Finland

	Worth threat	*Competence threat*	*Authenticity threat*
Female gender	−0.04	0.04	−0.01
Age (ref. 18–29)			
30–44	−0.22***	−0.20**	−0.18**
45–59	−0.26***	−0.20**	−0.22***
≥60	−0.34***	−0.27**	−0.32***
BA degree or higher	−0.15***	−0.12**	−0.13**
Entrepreneur	−0.23**	−0.23**	−0.21**
Supervisor	0.21***	0.18***	0.23***
Income (std)	−0.03	−0.05*	−0.06**
SME	−0.00	−0.00	−0.00
Field (ref. operational and coordination-intensive work)			
Market-oriented and performance-driven work	−0.08	0.01	−0.05
Technical and digital expertise	−0.01	0.07	0.01
Health and care professions	−0.14*	−0.11	−0.12*
Education and research	−0.09	−0.07	−0.07
Public administration and institutional professions	−0.08	0.06	−0.02
Cultural and expressive work	−0.16	−0.09	−0.08
Other	−0.09	−0.02	−0.08
Daily use of AI at work	0.03	0.05	−0.01
Organization uses AI	0.04	0.09*	0.05
Org. provides AI education	0.01	−0.02	0.01

Note: Random-effects regression models predicting perceived AI-related identity threat over time (*WorkAI* data, three waves, 2024–2025). Dependent variables (worth threat, competence threat, authenticity threat, range 4–28, see Appendix) are standardized (z-scores). Income is standardized. Models are based on three waves of panel data with 5009 observations from 2109 individuals. Statistical significance levels: *** $p < 0.001$, ** $p < 0.01$, * $p < 0.05$.

on role, position, and interpretation. Workers differ in how they interact with and interpret AI in relation to their professional values and prospects, and these differences are influenced by organizational hierarchies and workers' career stages. Identity threat does not necessarily equal vulnerability but also points to situations in which adaptation occurs and identity meanings are reassessed and potentially altered. However, these processes often involve emotional and psychological challenges. In the next section, we discuss the types of stressful experiences AI-related changes give rise to.

From Threat to Stress and Further Consequences

Challenges to professional identity may seem largely symbolic. However, when workers begin to question their value and meaning at work, this often translates into psychological and physical strain and uncertainty. In the context of technological change, such experiences have been widely examined under the concept of technostress, which refers to the stress arising from the introduction and intensification of technologies in work contexts (Ayyagari et al., 2011; Salo et al., 2022; Tarafdar et al., 2015). Technostress is typically associated with increased demands, constant connectivity, and a higher pace of work that tests workers' limits and can spill over from work to private life (Pirkkalainen et al., 2019; Tarafdar et al., 2015). In this landscape, AI represents a further intensification rather than a break from technological noise. AI systems increasingly modify and connect existing technologies, adding new layers of uncertainty, complexity, and perceived loss of control. As a result, stress may emerge not only from technology use itself but also from workers' sense of competence, autonomy, and identity.

Research on technostress has long examined how the introduction and proliferation of information and communication technologies induce strain for workers (Nisafani et al., 2020; Tarafdar et al., 2007). Early work defined technostress as stress or anxiety experienced when individuals struggle to cope with new technologies in a productive manner, highlighting stressors such as constant connectivity, information overload, role ambiguity, and loss of control (Brod, 1982). Subsequent research has demonstrated that technostress can arise in relation to both new and familiar technologies, for example, through software updates, changing interfaces, or new digital tools that alter established work practices (Shu et al., 2011; Tarafdar et al., 2007). More recent studies have suggested that technostress has become a persistent organizational challenge rather than a temporary adjustment problem (Pirkkalainen et al., 2019; Tarafdar et al., 2019; Tarafdar et al., 2020). A substantial body of research shows that technology-induced stressors can undermine well-being, reduce job satisfaction, and contribute to exhaustion, particularly when technological demands are perceived to exceed individuals' resources or available support (Ayyagari et al., 2011).

The outcomes of technostress are often described in psychological terms, such as anxiety, cognitive overload, and burnout, but they have also been found to manifest in physical or physiological symptoms, such as fatigue, headaches, and eyestrain (Nisafani et al., 2020). Experiencing technostress is also associated with lower productivity and decreased performance (Li & Wang, 2021; Tarafdar et al., 2015), making it a significant hindering factor in today's workers' overall job endurance and enjoyment. Several insights from the technostress literature are highly relevant in the age of AI. First, stress is not caused by technology per se but by the mismatch between human capacities and the demands that technology brings. Second, perception plays a role because technologies that are experienced as intrusive or not transparent tend to generate stronger stress reactions than those that are perceived as flexible or supportive.

AI introduces features that extend the scope of earlier technostress research. Unlike many previous digital tools, AI systems can participate directly in core tasks, judgment, and decision-making. As a result, AI-induced stress may stem not only from workload, complexity, or constant connectivity of new technology—and from demands of learning how to use it—but also from uncertainty and role boundaries and the future distribution of responsibility (Kumar et al., 2024). A recent study found that when people were working with AI and perceived a higher degree of AI control over decision-making, they reported higher stress, suggesting that AI also creates strain through perceived loss of autonomy (Klonek & Parker, 2025). However, the same study also showed that collaborative human–AI team processes were associated with lower stress, indicating that meaningful human involvement and coordination with AI can buffer some of the negative effects of AI control at work.

Table 4.2 presents findings based on our longitudinal *WorkAI* survey from Finland, investigating factors predicting AI-related stress in today's workplaces. The analyses concern three time points from autumn 2024 to autumn 2025. The table shifts the analytical focus from the predictors of AI-related identity threat (see Table 4.1) to its consequences. Table 4.2 uses these threat dimensions, together with social support at work and AI-use-related factors, to explain AI-related technostress. The fixed-effects models examined how within-person changes in AI-related identity threats are associated with changes in AI stress over time. Findings across three different models showed that over time, within-person changes in AI threats were significantly associated with a higher perception of stress. As shown in Table 4.2, one standard deviation increases in worth, competence, or authenticity threat are associated with a substantial increase in AI-related strain, with coefficients ranging from 1.43 to 1.50. The models accounted for several work-related and organizational factors, but in these

Table 4.2 Longitudinal fixed-effects models explaining AI stress in Finland

	Worth threat	*Competence threat*	*Authenticity threat*
Identity threat (std)	1.43***	1.47***	1.50***
Social support at work (std)	−0.15*	−0.18*	−0.19*
Positive AI attitude (std)	0.24**	0.22**	0.22**
Perceived AI competence (std)	0.28***	0.31***	0.31***
Daily use of AI at work	0.54*	0.48*	0.56**
Supervisor position	0.13	0.09	0.04
Income (std)	0.02	0.32	0.33
Organization uses AI	0.32	0.25	0.29
Org. provides AI education	−0.04	−0.002	−0.04

Note: The table reports the unstandardized coefficients (B) from the longitudinal fixed-effects regression models. The dependent variable is AI stress (range 3–21, see Appendix). Separate models are estimated for three dimensions of identity threat: worth threat, competence threat, and authenticity threat (see Appendix). Fixed-effects models control for all time-invariant individual characteristics by estimating within-person change over time. Variables marked (std) are standardized (mean = 0, SD = 1); all other predictors are binary indicators (0 = no, 1 = yes). All models adjust for social support at work, positive AI attitudes, perceived AI competence, daily use of AI at work, supervisory position, income, and organizational AI practices. The models are based on three waves of *WorkAI* survey data from Finland (N = 5023 observations from 2117 individuals). Statistical significance levels: *** $p < 0.001$, ** $p < 0.01$, * $p < 0.05$.

statistical models supervisory position, income, and organizational factors were not statistically significant.

The results from Table 4.2 also show that higher perceived AI competence and more frequent daily use of AI are associated with higher levels of AI-related stress. At first glance, this may appear counterintuitive, as technological anxiety is often assumed to be most prevalent among those who lack familiarity with new tools. Our findings suggest that experiences of stress are not confined to inexperienced users. These results show that higher engagement with AI technologies may amplify stressful experiences. In other words, using and understanding AI appears to increase exposure to identity-relevant tensions. One background reason might be that savvy users are more aware of how fast AI tools currently develop and how they invade new areas commonly considered human expertise only. In this sense, knowledge does not alleviate strain but may instead heighten it. More knowledgeable workers might also be more mindful of the risks of AI, such as ethics and data security, and thus feel conflicted about having to use it frequently.

One important and particularly relevant finding from our *WorkAI* longitudinal survey is that stress caused by AI at work likely has broader implications that extend beyond the demands of the occurring changes. We investigated the direct within- and between-person effects of AI stress and identity threats on work exhaustion. This result was based on the five-item exhaustion subscale of the Maslach Burnout Inventory–General Survey (Maslach et al., 2018). The findings from 2024 to 2025 showed that a within-person increase in AI-based stress is significantly associated with work exhaustion. Similar within-person effects of identity threats (worth, competence, and authenticity) were not found. However, we found that the between-person effects of identity threats, based on random-effects models, were also positively associated with work exhaustion. This suggests differences between individuals over time. Thus, in general, those who perceive more identity threats are also more likely to experience work exhaustion.

AI use is largely an individual behavior but, in workplaces, it is embedded in a shared work culture, norms, and guidelines that influence how it is evaluated and discussed. In these contexts, workers may increasingly assess their own competence as AI users in relation to their colleagues. Thus, an additional social psychological process that may contribute to work exhaustion is comparison among workers that can add pressure to some workers. Those who were high in comparison tendencies in the context of AI use at work reported higher levels of exhaustion in a recent study (Savolainen et al., 2026). Evaluation of competence and comparative pressure may thus present a pathway through which AI change adds strain. This further highlights the importance of supportive workplace environments and resources that can buffer strain and mitigate negative outcomes.

Coping and Managing Stress

We have previously seen that people perceive AI transformation at work as threatening and that it is associated with stress and further work exhaustion over time. Coping with such a threat is important. On the positive side, coping should be possible. An important lesson from research is that people are able to cope with extreme stressors (Bonanno, 2004; Bonanno et al., 2015; Chen & Bonanno, 2020). Resilience refers to positive adaptation and the ability to bounce back from even difficult situations (Bonanno et al., 2015; Herrman et al., 2011; Rutter, 2023). If a crisis is commonly shared between a larger group of individuals, prosocial behavior, social solidarity, and cooperation tend to increase, as shown, for example, in the aftermath of natural disasters or violent tragedies (Hawdon & Ryan, 2011; Norris et al., 2008). However, social and individual differences are persistent, and coping is often easier for those in better socioeconomic positions (Bonanno et al., 2007; McLeod & Kessler, 1990). Other relevant factors include family background, psychiatric history, and personality (Bonanno, 2004). Of the personality traits, neuroticism is found to correlate negatively with resilience (Oshio et al., 2018).

One of the most consistent roots of coping is the available social support (Cohen & Wills, 1985; Dalgard et al., 1995). Having strong social ties with family, friends, and colleagues is generally a very powerful resource for people and also responds to the social needs that people have (Leary & Baumeister, 1995). Particularly in the work context, there is extremely robust evidence of the protective role of social support at work in relation to stress and strain. Based on research, social support from colleagues and supervisors is associated with decreased stress, exhaustion, and strain, and social support also buffers the effects of work demands (Gilboa et al., 2008; Hämmig & Vetsch, 2021; Viswesvaran et al., 1999). This is also theoretically supported by different theories of stress and work demands that underline that social support at work is linked to better mental health and reduced burnout (Jolly et al., 2021). The most influential and widely used theoretical perspective is the Job Demands-resources Model (JD-R), which emphasizes the role of job resources, such as support from colleagues and supervisors, in sustaining work performance and well-being (Bakker & Demerouti, 2007). The protective function of social support is expected to hold across different types of demands, including technologically induced stressors. This suggests that social relationships remain a central coping resource, even under conditions of rapid digital and organizational change (Tarafdar et al., 2019).

We also saw this in our empirical findings, as demonstrated previously in Table 4.2, social support at work had a significant protective effect on AI stress in all models. In other words, within-person increases in social support over time were associated with a decrease in AI stress. We investigated this further by looking into the moderation between positive AI attitude and social support at work. This investigation showed that social support at work buffers AI-related stress. Positive attitude toward AI is associated with higher AI stress, but this association disappears when workers experience a high level of support from their colleagues and supervisors at work. We believe that this is an important finding in today's work life. Importantly, there were no significant protective factors in the organizational arrangements, such as organizations providing AI education. It seems that AI competence does not really protect workers from experiencing stress. In fact, in our analyses, it was shown that the within-person effect of identity threat on stress was stronger among participants with higher perceived AI competence. These results underline the nature of identity threats and stress. For individuals, it is easier to cope with stress related to AI transformation if they are socially supported. Our results align with earlier extensive work showing that social support from other people has a robust effect on the well-being and endurance of individuals (Leary & Baumeister, 1995; Cohen & McKay, 2020; Jolly et al., 2021). In the context of AI disruption, support from others also appears to play a key role.

It is natural that any work comes with a certain amount of stress, regardless of its source. However, workers have demonstrated resilience, and in addition to social support, they can draw from other positive resources that can support their coping and adaptation. One such resource is work engagement, which is an employee's positive, affective, and motivational state that involves vigor, dedication, and absorption (Bakker et al., 2008). It is often associated with the vision of energized and motivated workers who find meaning in what they do. Work engagement is further captured by the idea that when people are engaged, they are more deeply involved, their work feels less burdensome, and it is seen as more of a source of purpose. In research on working life, work engagement describes a positive psychological state characterized by absorption, dedication, and strong identification with one's work (Bakker et al., 2014; Leiter & Bakker, 2010). Work engagement does not indicate the opposite of stress; rather, it can coexist with demanding and changing work conditions. AI may either support or hinder work engagement, and understanding which of these trajectories becomes more likely, and under what circumstances, requires continuous timely research. At the same time, established research on engagement provides a strong foundation on which to build, highlighting the key supportive factors that typically sustain engagement.

We wanted to further understand whether work engagement could buffer against the negative effect that identity threats have on AI stress. Our fixed-effects models revealed a significant interaction between worth-related identity threats and work engagement. Increases in identity threats were strongly associated with higher AI stress. However, this association was weaker when higher work engagement was reported (see Fig. 4.1).

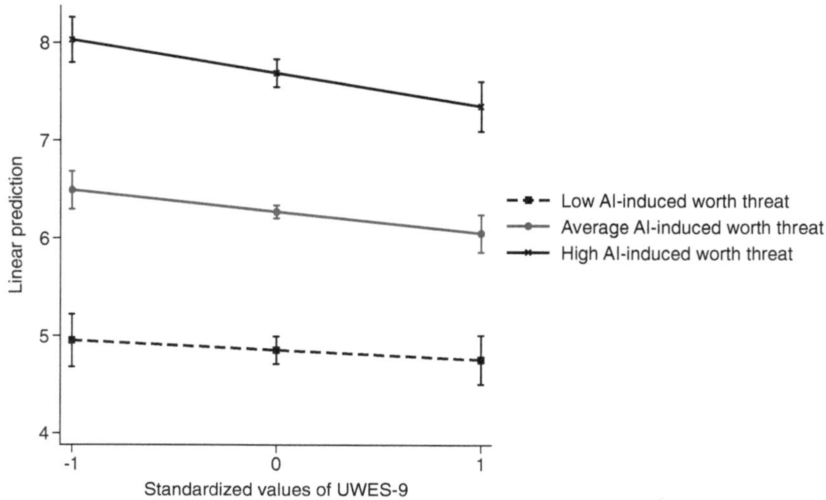

Fig. 4.1 Work engagement buffers the relationship between AI-based identity threat and AI stress in Finland. (Note: The figure displays the predicted values of AI stress (see Appendix) with 95% confidence intervals based on a longitudinal fixed-effects regression model. AI-related stress varies from 3 (very low) to 21 (very high). Predictions are shown for low (−1 SD), average (0), and high (+1 SD) levels of AI-related worth threat and work engagement (UWES-9, Seppälä et al., 2009). All estimates are based on within-person variation over time and are adjusted for the daily use of AI at work. The models are based on three waves of *WorkAI* data from Finland; 5023 observations from 2117 individuals during 2024–2025.)

This suggests that engagement functions as a psychological resource that buffers the stressful impact of identity threat.

Conclusion: Managing Strain in AI-shaped Work

This chapter examined how AI-driven change intersects with professional identity, stress, and coping mechanisms. Colombian author Gabriel García Márquez (2007) wrote in his renowned novel *Love in the Time of Cholera* that "human beings are not born once and for all on the day their mothers give birth to them, but that life obliges them over and over again to give birth to themselves" (p. 227). The author puts into words the notion that we see every day in people's lives: life pressures us into change in response to new circumstances and challenges. We do not always choose reinvention of ourselves or our identity, but often circumstances push people to adapt, grow, and rethink who they are.

AI represents a circumstance that presses workers into re-evaluating who they are as professionals and how they relate to their work. As we showed in this chapter, AI's impact is not limited to altered tasks or routines but touches workers' identities in ways that can generate uncertainty, strain, and the need for flexibility. Identity threat may arise when established roles, competence, or professional value are challenged, prompting a range of coping responses. At the same time, the findings we present underscore that these experiences are by no means uniform or predetermined but are more likely to emerge when certain personal and contextual factors co-occur. When AI identity threat and stress arise, they are often tied to how AI's implications are interpreted and how AI is embedded into work practices. Individuals can draw on personal resources, such as positive appraisal and social support, to cope effectively with the change. Coping itself is not limited to enduring change; it also involves learning, reframing, and engaging with AI in ways that allow preservation or even renewal of one's sense of professional meaning.

Maintaining work engagement is an important part of this adaptive process. It can function as a psychological resource that helps workers sustain motivation and meaning, even when work is transformed by AI. In practice, engagement is likely to be maintained when workers are able to maintain a sense of agency, have opportunities to influence how AI is used, and have fair expectations about their role. The extent to which workers believe they can learn, use, and influence AI systems in their work can impact how and whether identity threat and stress are experienced. The following chapter, therefore, focuses explicitly on self-efficacy, examining its role in shaping workers' responses to AI.

References

Ashforth, B. E., & Mael, F. (1989). Social identity theory and the organization. *Academy of Management Review, 14*(1), 20–39. https://doi.org/10.5465/amr.1989.4278999

Ayyagari, R., Grover, V., & Purvis, R. (2011). Technostress: Technological antecedents and implications. *MIS Quarterly, 35*(4), 831–858. https://doi.org/10.2307/41409963

Bakker, A. B., & Demerouti, E. (2007). The job demands-resources model: State of the art. *Journal of Managerial Psychology, 22*(3), 309–328. https://doi.org/10.1108/02683940710733115

Bakker, A. B., Demerouti, E., & Sanz-Vergel, A. I. (2014). Burnout and work engagement: The JD–R approach. *Annual Review of Organizational Psychology and Organizational Behavior, 1*(2014), 389–411. https://doi.org/10.1146/annurev-orgpsych-031413-091235

Bakker, A. B., Schaufeli, W. B., Leiter, M. P., & Taris, T. W. (2008). Work engagement: An emerging concept in occupational health psychology. *Work & Stress, 22*(3), 187–200. https://doi.org/10.1080/02678370802393649

Baumeister, R. F. (2022). *The self explained: Why and how we become who we are*. Guilford Publications.

Baumeister, R. F., & Bushman, B. J. (2020). *Social psychology and human nature*. Cengage Learning.

Bonanno, G. A. (2004). Loss, trauma, and human resilience: Have we underestimated the human capacity to thrive after extremely aversive events? *American Psychologist, 59*(1), 20–28. https://doi.org/10.1037/0003-066X.59.1.20

Bonanno, G. A., Galea, S., Bucciarelli, A., & Vlahov, D. (2007). What predicts psychological resilience after disaster? The role of demographics, resources, and life stress. *Journal of Consulting and Clinical Psychology, 75*(5), 671–682. https://doi.org/10.1037/0022-006X.75.5.671

Bonanno, G. A., Romero, S. A., & Klein, S. I. (2015). The temporal elements of psychological resilience: An integrative framework for the study of individuals, families, and communities. *Psychological Inquiry, 26*(2), 139–169. https://doi.org/10.1080/1047840X.2015.992677

Breakwell, G. M. (1986). *Coping with threatened identities*. Methuen.

Brod, C. (1982). Managing technostress: Optimizing the use of computer technology. *The Personnel Journal, 61*(10), 753–757.

Brown, R. (2020). The social identity approach: Appraising the Tajfellian legacy. *British Journal of Social Psychology, 59*(1), 5–25. https://doi.org/10.1111/bjso.12349

Chen, S., & Bonanno, G. A. (2020). Psychological adjustment during the global outbreak of COVID-19: A resilience perspective. *Psychological Trauma: Theory, Research, Practice, and Policy, 12*(S1), S51–S54. https://doi.org/10.1037/tra0000685

Chreim, S., Williams, B. E., & Hinings, C. R. (2007). Interlevel influences on the reconstruction of professional role identity. *Academy of Management Journal, 50*(6), 1515–1539. https://doi.org/10.5465/amj.2007.28226248

Cohen, S., & McKay, G. (2020). Social support, stress and the buffering hypothesis: A theoretical analysis. In A. Baum & S. E. Taylor (Eds.), *Handbook of psychology and health* (Vol. IV, pp. 253–267). Routledge.

Cohen, S., & Wills, T. A. (1985). Stress, social support, and the buffering hypothesis. *Psychological Bulletin, 98*, 310–357. https://doi.org/10.1037/0033-2909.98.2.310
Craig, K., Thatcher, J. B., & Grover, V. (2019). The IT identity threat: A conceptual definition and operational measure. *Journal of Management Information Systems, 36*(1), 259–288. https://doi.org/10.1080/07421222.2018.1550561
Crocetti, E., Albarello, F., Meeus, W., & Rubini, M. (2023). Identities: A developmental social-psychological perspective. *European Review of Social Psychology, 34*(1), 161–201. https://doi.org/10.1080/10463283.2022.2104987
Dalgard, O. S., Bjørk, S., & Tambs, K. (1995). Social support, negative life events and mental health. *The British Journal of Psychiatry, 166*, 29–34. https://doi.org/10.1192/bjp.166.1.29
García Márquez, G. (2007). *Love in the time of cholera*. (E. Grossman, Trans.). Knopf Doubleday Publishing Group.
Gilboa, S., Shirom, A., Fried, Y., & Cooper, C. (2008). A meta-analysis of work demand stressors and job performance: Examining main and moderating effects. *Personnel Psychology, 61*(2), 227–271. https://doi.org/10.1111/j.1744-6570.2008.00113.x
Guardian. (2023). *How Hollywood writers triumphed over AI—and why it matters*. https://www.theguardian.com/culture/2023/oct/01/hollywood-writers-strike-artificial-intelligence.
Hall, W. M., Schmader, T., & Croft, E. (2015). Engineering Exchanges: Daily Social Identity Threat Predicts Burnout Among Female Engineers. *Social Psychological & Personality Science, 6*(5), 528–534. https://doi.org/10.1177/1948550615572637
Hämmig, O., & Vetsch, A. (2021). Stress-buffering and health-protective effect of job autonomy, good working climate, and social support at work among health care workers in Switzerland. *Journal of Occupational and Environmental Medicine, 63*(12), e918–e924. https://doi.org/10.1097/JOM.0000000000002404
Harré, R. (1983). *Personal being: A theory for individual psychology*. Basil Blackwell.
Haslam, S. A. (2012). *Psychology in organizations: The social identity approach* (2nd ed.). SAGE.
Hawdon, J., & Ryan, J. (2011). Social relations that generate and sustain solidarity after a mass tragedy. *Social Forces, 89*(4), 1363–1384. https://doi.org/10.1093/sf/89.4.1363
Heiskari, M., Celuch, M., Koivula, A., Savolainen, I., & Oksanen, A. (2025). Technological identity and basic psychological needs in the use of new technologies: A two-wave cross-national survey study. *International Journal of Information Management, 84*(October 2025), 102926. https://doi.org/10.1016/j.ijinfomgt.2025.102926

Herrman, H., Stewart, D. E., Diaz-Granados, N., Berger, E. L., Jackson, B., & Yuen, T. (2011). What is resilience? *The Canadian Journal of Psychiatry, 56*(5), 258–265. https://doi.org/10.1177/070674371105600504

Inglehart, R., & Welzel, C. (2005). *Modernization, cultural change, and democracy: The human development sequence.* Cambridge University Press.

Jenkins, R. (2014). *Social identity.* Routledge.

Jolly, P. M., Kong, D. T., & Kim, K. Y. (2021). Social support at work: An integrative review. *Journal of Organizational Behavior, 42*(2), 229–251. https://doi.org/10.1002/job.2485

Jussupow, E., Spohrer, K., & Heinzl, A. (2022). Identity threats as a reason for resistance to artificial intelligence: Survey study with medical students and professionals. *JMIR Formative Research, 6*(3), e28750. https://doi.org/10.2196/28750

Kitayama, S., Markus, H. R., Matsumoto, H., & Norasakkunkit, V. (1997). Individual and collective processes in the construction of the self: Self-enhancement in the United States and self-criticism in Japan. *Journal of Personality and Social Psychology, 72*(6), 1245–1267.

Klonek, F., & Parker, S. (2025). Does AI at work increase stress? Text mining social media about human–AI team processes and AI control. *Journal of Organizational Behavior.* https://doi.org/10.1002/job.70000

Kumar, A., Krishnamoorthy, B., & Bhattacharyya, S. S. (2024). Machine learning and artificial intelligence-induced technostress in organizations: A study on automation-augmentation paradox with socio-technical systems as coping mechanisms. *International Journal of Organizational Analysis, 32*(4), 681–701. https://doi.org/10.1108/IJOA-01-2023-3581

Leary, M. R., & Baumeister, R. F. (1995). The need to belong. *Psychological Bulletin, 117*(3), 497–529. https://doi.org/10.4324/9780367198459-REPRW57-1

Leiter, M. P., & Bakker, A. B. (2010). Work engagement: Introduction. In A. B. Bakker & M. P. Leiter (Eds.), *Work engagement: A handbook of essential theory and research* (pp. 1–9). Psychology Press.

Li, L., & Wang, X. (2021). Technostress inhibitors and creators and their impacts on university teachers' work performance in higher education. *Cognition, Technology & Work, 23*(2), 315–330. https://doi.org/10.1007/s10111-020-00625-0

Markus, H. R., & Kitayama, S. (2010). Cultures and selves: A cycle of mutual constitution. *Perspectives on Psychological Science, 5*(4), 420–430. https://doi.org/10.1177/1745691610375557

Maslach, C., Jackson, S. E., & Leiter, M. P. (2018). *Maslach burnout inventory manual fourth edition.* Mind Garden. https://www.mindgarden.com/312-mbi-general-survey

McLeod, J. D., & Kessler, R. C. (1990). Socioeconomic status differences in vulnerability to undesirable life events. *Journal of Health and Social Behavior, 31*(2), 162–172. https://doi.org/10.2307/2137170

Mirbabaie, M., Brünker, F., Möllmann Frick, N. R., & Stieglitz, S. (2022). The rise of artificial intelligence–understanding the AI identity threat at the workplace. *Electronic Markets, 32*(1), 73–99. https://doi.org/10.1007/s12525-021-00496-x

Miscenko, D., & Day, D. V. (2016). Identity and identification at work. *Organizational Psychology Review, 6*(3), 215–247. https://doi.org/10.1177/2041386615584009

Nisafani, A. S., Kiely, G., & Mahony, C. (2020). Workers' technostress: A review of its causes, strains, inhibitors, and impacts. *Journal of Decision Systems, 29*(sup1), 243–258. https://doi.org/10.1080/12460125.2020.1796286

Norris, F. H., Stevens, S. P., Pfefferbaum, B., Wyche, K. F., & Pfefferbaum, R. L. (2008). Community resilience as a metaphor, theory, set of capacities, and strategy for disaster readiness. *American Journal of Community Psychology, 41*(1–2), 127–150. https://doi.org/10.1007/s10464-007-9156-6

Oshio, A., Taku, K., Hirano, M., & Saeed, G. (2018). Resilience and Big Five personality traits: A meta-analysis. *Personality and Individual Differences, 127*, 54–60. https://doi.org/10.1016/j.paid.2018.01.048

Pirkkalainen, H., Salo, M., Tarafdar, M., & Makkonen, M. (2019). Deliberate or instinctive? Proactive and reactive coping for technostress. *Journal of Management Information Systems, 36*(4), 1179–1212. https://doi.org/10.1080/07421222.2019.1661092

Rutter, M. (2023). Resilience: Some conceptual considerations. In V. E. Cree & T. McCulloch (Eds.), *Social Work* (pp. 122–127). Routledge. https://doi.org/10.4324/9781003178699-23

Salo, M., Pirkkalainen, H., Chua, C. E. H., & Koskelainen, T. (2022). Formation and mitigation of technostress in the personal use of IT. *MIS Quarterly, 46*(2), 1073–1108. https://doi.org/10.25300/MISQ/2022/14950

Savela, N., Kaakinen, M., Ellonen, N., & Oksanen, A. (2021). Sharing a work team with robots: The negative effect of robot co-workers on in-group identification with the work team. *Computers in Human Behavior, 115*, 106585. https://doi.org/10.1016/j.chb.2020.106585

Savolainen, I., Brailovskaia, J., Sirola, A., Celuch, M., & Oksanen, A. (2025). Just a few more minutes: Longitudinal and cross-national perspectives on the role of online identity bubbles in addictive internet use. *Computers in Human Behavior, 165*(April 2025), 108555. https://doi.org/10.1016/j.chb.2025.108555

Savolainen, I., Osma, T., Grönroos, R., Heiskari, M., & Oksanen, A. (2026). Social comparison contributes to work exhaustion in the context of workplace

AI use: A three-wave follow-up study of Finnish workers. *SSM-Population Health*, https://doi.org/10.1016/j.ssmph.2026.101945

Schwartz, S. J. (2001). The evolution of Eriksonian and, neo-Eriksonian identity theory and research: A review and integration. *Identity, 1*(1), 7–58. https://doi.org/10.1207/S1532706XSCHWARTZ

Seppälä, P., Mauno, S., Feldt, T., Hakanen, J., Kinnunen, U., Tolvanen, A., & Schaufeli, W. (2009). The construct validity of the Utrecht Work Engagement Scale: Multisample and longitudinal evidence. *Journal of Happiness Studies, 10*(4), 459–481. https://doi.org/10.1007/s10902-008-9100-y

Shu, Q., Tu, Q., & Wang, K. (2011). The impact of computer self-efficacy and technology dependence on computer-related technostress: A social cognitive theory perspective. *International Journal of Human-Computer Interaction, 27*(10), 923–939. https://doi.org/10.1080/10447318.2011.555313

Tarafdar, M., Cooper, C. L., & Stich, J.-F. (2019). The technostress trifecta—Techno eustress, techno distress and design. *Information Systems Journal, 29*(1), 6–42. https://doi.org/10.1111/isj.12169

Tarafdar, M., Pirkkalainen, H., Salo, M., & Makkonen, M. (2020). Taking on the "dark side"—Coping with technostress. *IT Professional, 22*(6), 82–89. https://doi.org/10.1109/MITP.2020.2977343

Tarafdar, M., Pullins, E. B., & Ragu-Nathan, T. S. (2015). Technostress: Negative effect on performance and possible mitigations. *Information Systems Journal, 25*(2), 103–132. https://doi.org/10.1111/isj.12042

Tarafdar, M., Tu, Q., Ragu-Nathan, B. S., & Ragu-Nathan, T. S. (2007). The impact of technostress on role stress and productivity. *Journal of Management Information Systems, 24*(1), 301–328. https://doi.org/10.2753/MIS0742-1222240109

Triandis, H. C. (2018). *Individualism and collectivism*. Routledge.

Viswesvaran, C., Sanchez, J. I., & Fisher, J. (1999). The role of social support in the process of work stress: A meta-analysis. *Journal of Vocational Behavior, 54*(2), 314–334. https://doi.org/10.1006/jvbe.1998.1661

Walsh, K., & Gordon, J. R. (2008). Creating an individual work identity. *Human Resource Management Review, 18*(1), 46–61. https://doi.org/10.1016/j.hrmr.2007.09.001

Yang, N., & Zhang, R. (2023). Under threat: Emotional and behavioral responses to occupational identity threat. *Journal of Management & Organization, 29*(3), 464–480. Article 1833367221000535. https://doi.org/10.1017/jmo.2021.53

CHAPTER 5

AI Self-efficacy at Work

Abstract This chapter examines the well-being implications of AI implementation, focusing on work engagement and the critical role of perceived self-efficacy in workers' AI adoption. Although AI can enhance efficiency and create new opportunities for learning, it can also challenge workers' sense of competence and control, making psychological resources central to successful adaptation. Drawing on longitudinal evidence, we show how AI-related benefits influence work engagement over time, capturing the dynamic process through which employees adjust to technological changes. We consider self-efficacy to be a key psychological resource that facilitates the successful uptake of AI tools. This reflects workers' perceived capability to learn about and use AI systems and strengthens through ongoing interaction and experience with them. By identifying factors that explain changes in AI learning readiness and self-efficacy over time, this chapter offers timely empirical insights into how worker well-being can be supported during transformation. We highlight workers' agency rather than viewing them as passive recipients of AI implementation.

Keywords Self-efficacy • Work engagement • Well-being • Resources • Learning

A. Oksanen, I. Savolainen, *AI Disruption at Work*, Palgrave Advances in Work and Organizational Psychology,
https://doi.org/10.1007/978-3-032-35207-1_5

The history of workplace technology implementation shows that successful adoption does not merely rely on system design and function. What has been a great testament to people's adaptability and flexibility is that technologies that initially appear complex have repeatedly become ordinary tools once people have learned how to use them. From early office machines to personal computers and larger enterprise-wide software, workers have often acquired new technological skills faster than expected by their peers of the time. The relatively fast learning was not necessarily due to the technologies being intuitive or easy to use from the get-go but because of routines, available training, and social support and learning that smoothed the implementation process.

What has changed in recent decades is, of course, the advancement of technologies and also the frequency and pace in which transition occurs. As work becomes increasingly characterized by rapid digital and AI-related change, workers are required to adapt to new tools and to do so both promptly and under uncertainty. With AI and automation accelerating the way and routine at which tasks, roles, and expectations evolve, individuals' capacity to learn, adjust, and remain effective in their work becomes a race. In such a context, the available social and psychological resources become particularly consequential. In the previous chapter, we saw that AI can threaten identity and increase strain. Building on this background, in this chapter, we move on to investigate under what conditions AI supports motivation, well-being, and sustainable engagement at work.

We will discuss in more detail the role of self-efficacy in these processes—in other words, the belief that individuals hold about their ability to successfully perform the required actions to achieve the desired outcomes. In work settings, self-efficacy is crucial in influencing how employees approach challenges, persist in the face of challenge, and respond to change. Self-efficacy is not so much reflective of an individual's objective skills, but it covers a sense of perceived ability and capability that relate to motivation, effort, and resilience (Bandura, 2023; Bartimote-Aufflick et al., 2016; Consiglio et al., 2016; Oksanen et al., 2026). In a situation as demonstrated by today's AI emergence and technological demand, workers who believe they can master new tools and changing processes are more likely to engage with the change more proactively and efficiently (Kim et al., 2024; Kim & Lee, 2024). Those who doubt their abilities, on the other hand, may experience stress or avoidant behaviors.

Research on self-efficacy in work and technology contexts has a long tradition. Prior studies have examined self-efficacy in domain-specific settings, including computer self-efficacy (Compeau et al., 2015), digital skills (Ulfert-Blank & Schmidt, 2022), and, more recently, robot use (Latikka et al., 2023) and the use of AI (Oksanen et al., 2026). Across these domains, self-efficacy has been linked to technology acceptance, learning, and performance, reflecting individuals' perceived ability to understand, benefit from, and operate technological systems. When workers feel they can master new tools, they are more likely to approach change with motivation and sustained work engagement. In this chapter, we will present cross-national results from the *Self and Technology* data and national findings from *WorkAI* data, demonstrating how work engagement and self-efficacy are experienced and relate to work outcomes in the AI context.

Work Engagement in the Age of AI

Work engagement is one of the most central concepts of work well-being in academic and popular literature and discussions. In academic research, the concept was introduced by Kahn (1990) and later developed further through expanding work–life research (Bakker et al., 2008; Knight et al., 2017; Lesener et al., 2020; Schaufeli & Bakker, 2013). Work engagement has its roots in positive psychology and has a theoretical basis in the job demands-resources (JD-R) model (Bakker et al., 2014). The JD-R model enables researchers to understand the negative and positive aspects of work (Bakker et al., 2023; Lesener et al., 2019). The previous chapter discussed the side of exhaustion. On the other hand, engagement is an employee's positive and long-lasting psychological state related to work in which the employee feels vigorous, dedicated, and absorbed in their work; thus, the concept embodies the positive side of employee well-being expansively (Schaufeli & Bakker, 2004; Schaufeli et al., 2002). Work engagement is driven by high job resources (i.e., various physical, psychological, organizational, and social features of work, such as autonomy, performance feedback, and social support, which intrinsically motivate workers to do the work; Bakker, 2011; Demerouti et al., 2001; Schaufeli & Bakker, 2004).

Over the past few years, work practices in various occupational fields have taken a rapid shift toward more technology-oriented ways of accomplishing work (Nagel, 2020; Savolainen et al., 2026; Vargo et al., 2021). The recent technological leap has increased interest in studying digital communication at work and its relation to enhanced work engagement

(Cheng et al., 2020; Oksa et al., 2021; Sun et al., 2022; Ye et al., 2024; Zhao & Yu, 2023), as well as its association with job satisfaction (Demircioglu, 2018; Liang et al., 2021; Wang et al., 2021; Zhang et al., 2022). Studies have suggested that digital tools can function as job resources and demands, depending on how they are implemented and experienced (Li et al., 2025; Poirier & Gelin, 2025). Technologies that enhance worker autonomy, provide feedback, or reduce workload are associated with higher engagement, as they free cognitive resources and enable more meaningful task allocation and involvement. However, constant connectivity, rapid change, and expectations of increased performance may also add pressure and undermine engagement by reducing sense of control.

Although the current AI diffusion is global, its rate and workplace implementation are highly tied to national contexts, including labor market structures, institutional protocols, and cultural and societal norms surrounding technology and work. Differences exist in regulatory environments and managerial practices, which can influence whether AI is introduced as mandatory or optional or whether it is a supportive tool or a monitoring system, all of which can contribute differently to worker outcomes in terms of engagement, resources, and demands. Research is increasingly recognizing these contextual significances, but comparative studies are still somewhat limited, particularly in the rapidly evolving context of GenAI. The *Self and Technology* data offer valuable insights into what factors relate to work engagement across cultural and geographical settings.

Table 5.1 presents regression models explaining work engagement in 12 countries. We found that across all countries, perceived happiness emerged as the strongest and most consistent predictor of engagement. This means that happy people feel stronger engagement in their work. We also measured social ties with friends utilizing three items adapted from the Social and Emotional Loneliness Scale for Adults (DiTommaso et al., 2004). These refer also to available social support, and we found them a robust predictor of work engagement. These findings highlight that affective resources play a central role in workers' well-being at work. The relationship between happiness and work well-being is also likely reciprocal, such that happiness supports positive work experiences, and supportive, meaningful work can also contribute to happiness. Either way, this points to the importance of maintaining positive affect and supportive work conditions.

Table 5.1 Linear regression models explaining work engagement in 12 countries

Country	*AI use at work*	*Pos. AI attitude*	*AILRSE*	*New tech user identity*	*Supportive friends*	*Happi-ness*	*Adj. model R^2*
Australia	0.00	0.04	0.10	−0.03	0.10*	0.36***	0.23
Brazil	0.03	0.08	0.05	0.08*	0.12**	0.29***	0.22
Finland	−0.03	0.08	0.10*	0.05	0.10	0.33***	0.20
France	0.02	0.16**	0.01	−0.05	0.11*	0.29***	0.15
Germany	0.02	−0.02	0.03	0.09	0.16**	0.19***	0.10
Ireland	−0.05	0.01	0.10	0.05	0.26***	0.25***	0.17
Italy	−0.01	0.01	0.05	0.05	0.16**	0.34***	0.24
Japan	0.07	−0.01	0.01	0.11*	0.25***	0.23***	0.24
Poland	0.02	−0.03	0.09	0.04	0.13*	0.29***	0.17
Portugal	0.08*	−0.02	0.13**	0.04	0.11**	0.23***	0.17
South Africa	−0.03	0.07	0.05	0.12**	0.05	0.24***	0.12
United States	−0.06	0.03	0.16**	0.03	0.11**	0.31***	0.18

Note. The table reports standardized beta coefficients (β) from linear regression models predicting work engagement, measured with UWES-3 (range 0–18, Schaufeli et al., 2019). All models were estimated separately for each country and adjusted for age, gender, and education. Robust standard errors were used. Higher values indicate higher levels of work engagement. Adjusted R^2 indicates the proportion of variance in work engagement explained by each model. Statistical significance levels: *** $p < 0.001$, ** $p < 0.01$, * $p < 0.05$.

Technology-related factors were less consistently associated with work engagement. For instance, AI use at work itself was not associated with engagement in any country sample, except Portugal, where it had a small positive effect. However, two factors reflecting workers' orientation toward technology; AI learning readiness self-efficacy and identity as a new technology user, had positive associations with engagement in some countries. We measured AI learning readiness self-efficacy with the AILRSE-5 scale (Oksanen et al., 2026) which captures individuals' perceived capability to learn and use AI tools. New technology user identity reflects in-group identification with other new technology users (Heiskari et al., 2025). These results are important in showing that despite ongoing AI disruption at work, technologies do not determine how people feel about their work. From a broader view, it is perhaps more important how individuals perceive their capabilities and identities in relation to technological change.

Overall, our findings complement previous research on work well-being, which suggests that although technologies can introduce new demands and opportunities, their effects are often not direct or even consistent. Instead, they are filtered through workers' appraisals and resources, as well as through the surrounding work context. As our analysis indicates, technology-related factors seem more situational and, at times, country-specific, such as positive attitudes being salient mostly in France. In contrast, social resources are a more universal predictor, tapping into the human side of dealing with new technologies. The psychosocial conditions with which AI is introduced and experienced give employers and organizations valuable tools to work with. In the near future, it is likely that supportive engagement will increasingly stem from workers and AI efficiently performing tasks together. This, however, may depend on whether workers perceive and directly experience tangible gains from AI. Recent research also points toward an optimal level of AI adoption at which workers' job satisfaction improves; both low and high levels of adoption were found to be associated with reduced job satisfaction, whereas a moderate level of adoption was related to greater satisfaction (Schulz et al., 2026). In the next section, we analyze and discuss a variety of perceived gains that can support engagement.

Engagement as a Function of Perceived Gains

Thus far, we have shown how AI-related integration and changes to work can impact and often undermine work engagement. However, an equally important question is when and under what conditions workers perceive technological change and AI as beneficial. From the perspective of individuals' appraisals, engagement is more likely to occur when new demands are interpreted as opportunities (Bakker & Sanz-Vergel, 2013; Crawford et al., 2010; Kim & Beehr, 2020). In this sense, engagement can be understood as reflecting perceived gains, whether in competence, autonomy, skills, or status. Perceived gains from AI may take many different forms. Research has suggested that workers often associate AI with enhanced efficiency and reduced workload, freeing time for creative exploration or expanding skillsets (Bankins et al., 2024; Ranganathan & Ye, 2026). These experiences can strengthen a sense of mastery and control, which will support motivation and involvement in work. At best, when AI is appraised as a tool that complements professional roles rather than competes with them, its benefits can extend to renewed interest and dedication to work.

Importantly, perceived gains are socially shaped and subjective. The same AI systems may be experienced in a positive and empowering light by one worker and threatening by another, depending on role, organizational context, or prior experience and competence. Engagement in AI-mediated work, therefore, balances hindrance and support appraisals. When perceived gains outweigh perceived losses, workers may be more likely to sustain dedication toward and absorption in their work. On the other hand, when perception is dominated by losses, engagement may suffer. Considering work engagement as an outcome gained from AI-related benefits has important practical implications for organizations navigating AI implementation; it highlights factors that can be strengthened through learning opportunities, social support, policy changes, and guideline development or through efforts shifting mindsets of AI use at work.

Table 5.2 shows hybrid (within-between) models of how AI-related benefits explain work engagement over time. These are based on the *WorkAI* longitudinal survey findings from Finland from 2024 to 2025 over a period of 12 months. Perceived AI-related benefits were positively associated with work engagement but mostly at the between-person level. Employees who, on average, perceived AI as accelerating work, improving quality, supporting learning, or enhancing performance reported higher

Table 5.2 Within- and between-person effects of perceived AI benefits on work engagement in Finland

	AI speeds up work	*AI automates tasks*	*AI helps to learn*	*AI improves quality*	*AI improves performance*
Within-person effect	0.14	0.29	0.36	0.63*	0.56*
Between-person effect	1.22***	0.66*	1.19***	1.20***	1.16***

Note: The table reports coefficients from hybrid (within–between) mixed-effects linear models predicting work engagement, measured with UWES-9 (range 0–54, Seppälä et al., 2009). The models simultaneously estimate within-person effects and between-person effects. AI-related benefit variables were standardized (mean = 0, SD = 1), and the coefficients indicate the change in work engagement associated with a one standard deviation increase in the predictor. We utilized *WorkAI* longitudinal survey data with three waves in 2024–2025. All models adjust for age, gender, education, supervisory position, and social support. The models included 2663 observations from 1357 individuals. Statistical significance levels: *** $p < 0.001$, ** $p < 0.01$, * $p < 0.05$.

overall work engagement compared to others. These between-person effects were consistently positive and statistically significant across the models. We also found some within-person effects. Short-term increases in perceived improvements in quality and performance were significantly associated with higher engagement. The models were adjusted for a number of sociodemographic factors and social support received at work. Although not reported in the table, social support emerged as the strongest and most consistent predictor of engagement. Within-person increases in support and higher average levels of support were strongly associated with higher work engagement. The results suggest that stable perceptions of AI as beneficial are closely linked to engagement.

These fresh insights are also rather intuitive; they center on core factors that help people do their work better (i.e., greater efficiency, lesser routine tasks, learning and skill development, and improvements in quality and performance). These mechanisms also align with recent evidence that AI-assisted work can support productive flow. When AI removes obstacles that slow one down and strengthens effectiveness, workers may choose to do more, not because of external requirements or expectations but because they feel more productive and the work feels more achievable (Ranganathan & Ye, 2026).

Our data followed workers over a year in 2024–2025, during which individuals' perceptions or experiences of AI-related gains may not yet have shifted dramatically. Still, we found meaningful within-person effects, suggesting that internal changes in experienced gains can translate into higher engagement over time. Stronger between-person associations may reflect relatively stable differences between workers in how beneficial AI feels in their tasks and roles. The broader implication is encouraging, as AI can be leveraged to support work engagement, which is a major resource in today's competitive and performance-driven working life. The remaining challenge and a central practical question for organizations, however, is how to create conditions under which such gains can be broadly accessible and distributed across roles and worker groups rather than remaining concentrated and benefiting only those who are better positioned to take advantage of them.

These considerations and results highlight the importance of interdisciplinary approaches. Supporting work engagement and future worker well-being requires perspectives that cut across the social and health sciences, communication and management studies, information technology and data science, and public policy, among other fields. As AI continues to change work in fast and even unpredictable ways, the conditions to sustain motivation, job satisfaction, and meaning cannot be addressed solely through digital design, organizational guidelines, or individual adoption. Instead, effective and responsible solutions depend on comprehensive multidisciplinary knowledge and collaboration that can ensure there is a meaningful realistic link in how AI systems are developed and subsequently governed, implemented, and used in workplaces.

This type of collaboration could, for example, be realized through AI developers working with worker representatives and human resources (HR) professionals making practice- and research-informed decisions when designing and implementing AI systems. Instead of introducing generic tools, AI solutions could be tailored to specific occupational contexts, incorporating feedback received about their effects on workers and work processes. Approaching the AI challenge in this manner could mean a potential paradigm shift in which AI would not be viewed purely as a tool but as a sociotechnical system.

AI Self-efficacy as a Central Psychological Resource

Most people likely remember the first time they had to use a device or tool that felt strange or intimidating at the time, whether a spreadsheet or a new system login. Since then, usage has become easier and more routine-like, not so much because the technology has changed but because of the user's sense of readiness, the belief that "I can figure this out" supported their learning and continued usage. AI introduces a similar threshold experience in today's workplaces. However, as we have seen in the earlier chapters, current AI is unprecedented as a technology both in scale and the range it covers. Thus, the learning process may seem different as technology evolves, and even individuals who may not have been anticipating its need or use in their own work are faced with AI. Differences in learning readiness and confidence are likely to influence who experiments with AI, who is more likely to integrate it, and who opts out.

Self-efficacy theory proposes that individuals form beliefs about how capable they are of successfully executing tasks and actions to achieve desired outcomes (Bandura, 1997). Although the theory was not originally developed in the context of technology, it has become widely applied in different domains, including research on the use of specified technologies, such as computer-use self-efficacy (Compeau & Higgins, 1995), internet-use self-efficacy (Eastin & LaRose, 2000), and robot-use self-efficacy (Latikka et al., 2019). In these contexts, self-efficacy is not simply used to describe users' knowledge but their perceived ability and confidence to use technology successfully. The rise of AI has also created the need for measures that assess self-efficacy related to its use. Although some existing technology-related self-efficacy measures can be applied to AI to a certain extent, they do not adequately capture the unique characteristics of AI, highlighting the need for tailored assessments that target AI-specific features.

New ways to assess AI self-efficacy are emerging (Wang & Chuang, 2024). However, a large portion of the measures currently available, although relevant, have often been designed for specific contexts, such as education, limiting their applicability to broader groups, especially cross-nationally. At the same time, many existing scales focus on skills or knowledge and assess them using lengthy item sets. In the landscape of these existing tools, we responded to this measurement need with a new approach and developed and validated the five-item AI Learning Readiness Self-Efficacy (AILRSE-5) scale utilizing 17 samples from 12 countries (N = 20,173; Oksanen et al., 2026). Unlike other measures, the AILRSE-5 addresses individuals' perceived ability to learn and understand how AI works and how to use it independently. In today's working life, AI skills are crucial, involving the ability to use and apply its many tools and the ability to critically evaluate inputs, distinguish information from misinformation, and use the tools safely. Here, we examine different psychosocial factors and how they relate to one's perceived ability to learn and use AI.

Table 5.3 shows the results of the regression models for AI learning readiness self-efficacy across 12 countries. The models focused on workers only. The results are highly, and perhaps surprisingly, consistent. In all the models, positive attitudes toward AI are the strongest predictor of self-efficacy, with standardized coefficients ranging from $\beta = 0.22$ (Japan) to $\beta = 0.58$ (Germany). This suggests that confidence in learning and using AI is strongly anchored in how positively individuals evaluate these technologies. Our results further evidence that identity factors are important in explaining AI use and related factors. We found that having an identity as a new technology user is positively associated with AI learning readiness self-efficacy in most countries and with relatively strong correlations in some of them, for example, Japan ($\beta = 0.38$) and France ($\beta = 0.24$). These results suggest that identifying oneself as a technologically oriented person supports workers' AI learning and further use. Furthermore, work engagement has a positive association with AI learning readiness self-efficacy in

Table 5.3 Linear regression models explaining AI learning readiness self-efficacy in 12 countries (standardized beta regression coefficients)

	Positive AI attitude	*New tech user Identity*	*Autonomy frustration*	*Competence frustration*	*Relatedness satisfaction*	*Work engagement*	*Adj. R^2*
Australia	0.47***	0.15**	0.20***	−0.26***	0.02	0.07**	0.45
Brazil	0.49***	0.18***	0.00	−0.15***	0.04	0.02	0.47
Finland	0.32***	0.12	0.09	−0.31***	0.09	0.09*	0.28
France	0.42***	0.24***	0.19***	−0.23***	-0.07	0.03	0.44
Germany	0.58***	−0.02	0.15*	−0.28***	0.08	0.05	0.43
Ireland	0.44***	0.12*	0.05	−0.24**	0.09	0.06	0.36
Italy	0.40***	0.20***	0.05	−0.21***	0.08	0.04	0.39
Japan	0.22***	0.38***	0.16***	−0.23***	0.03	0.08**	0.49
Poland	0.40***	0.11	0.07	−0.26***	0.11	0.11*	0.34
Portugal	0.50***	0.14***	0.09*	−0.25***	0.01	0.09**	0.40
South Africa	0.43***	0.17***	0.08	−0.19***	0.10	0.02	0.48
United States	0.44***	0.15***	0.14*	−0.21***	0.05	0.09**	0.38

Note: The table reports standardized beta coefficients (β) from country-specific linear regression models predicting AI learning readiness self-efficacy (AILRSE-5, range 5–35; see Appendix). The models include only participants who are working. All continuous predictors were standardized prior to estimation. The models include positive AI attitude, new technology user identity, autonomy frustration, competence frustration, relatedness satisfaction, and work engagement as predictors. The models are also adjusted for age, gender, and education (not shown). Adjusted R^2 values are reported. Statistical significance levels: *** $p < 0.001$, ** $p < 0.01$, * $p < 0.05$.

some countries (e.g., Australia, Finland, Japan, Poland, Portugal, and the United States). This could suggest that energized and dedicated workers may feel more capable of learning AI.

In Table 5.3, we also see evidence of basic psychological needs. These refer to universal human needs, as described by Self-determination Theory (SDT; Deci & Ryan, 2008, Ryan & Deci, 2000; Ryan & Deci, 2017). These basic needs are autonomy, competence, and relatedness. Autonomy refers to an individual's sense of choice or control over what happens in their life; competence refers to a sense of capability and mastery in domains that are meaningful to them, and relatedness refers to feelings of belonging and connection with others. When these basic psychological needs are satisfied, individuals are more likely to experience well-being, higher motivation, and overall thriving. When needs are frustrated, individuals may experience negative outcomes, such as stress or lower life satisfaction (Vansteenkiste et al., 2020). Basic psychological needs have broad applicability, and emerging research is also beginning to acknowledge their relevance in relation to AI (e.g., Bergdahl et al., 2023; Kaya et al., 2025).

Our models measured technology-related frustration and satisfaction of basic psychological needs. The results showed that competence frustration is remarkably consistently negatively associated with AI learning readiness self-efficacy. In every country, a higher frustration of competence needs is associated with lower AI learning readiness (βs between −0.15 and −0.31). This indicates that feelings of inadequacy could substantially undermine confidence in engaging with AI. However, autonomy frustration displayed smaller and less consistent positive effects, reaching significance in several countries (e.g., Australia, France, and Japan), whereas relatedness satisfaction is generally weak and nonsignificant.

Using the *WorkAI* data, we analyzed longitudinally what explains high AI learning readiness self-efficacy in the year 2025 in Finland. Our hybrid (within–between) panel model included sociodemographic and organizational factors. We further wanted to understand the role of social support and transformational leadership. With transformational leadership, we refer to a style of leading that inspires, motivates, and supports employees in innovative thinking (Carless et al., 2000). Our longitudinal results (see Table 5.4) show that leadership and social support play a meaningful role in AI learning readiness self-efficacy over time. At the within-person level, increases in transformational leadership (and social support at work) were associated with increases in individuals' AI learning readiness self-efficacy. This suggests that when employees experience more supportive and inspiring leadership or stronger workplace support than usual, their confidence in learning and adapting to AI also increases. At the between-person level, employees working in organizations that use AI reported substantially higher AI learning readiness self-efficacy, and higher average levels of workplace support were also positively associated with self-efficacy. Among the background factors, younger employees, men, and those with a university degree reported higher levels of AI learning readiness self-efficacy.

Table 5.5 shows hybrid panel regression models that focus on workers who utilize AI-related tools at work. We investigated the role of AI learning readiness self-efficacy in the use of AI tools that can be categorized into (1) generative AI tools (e.g., chatbots), (2) analytical and predictive tools (e.g., predictive analytics), and (3) embedded enterprise AI systems (e.g., decision support). Our results indicate that AI learning readiness

Table 5.4 Within- and between-person predictors of AI learning readiness self-efficacy in Finland

	Within-person effects	*Between-person effects*
Transformational leadership (std)	0.07*	0.05
Social support at work (std)	0.08*	0.08**
Organization uses AI (0/1)	0.10	0.45***
Organization provides AI education (0/1)	−0.02	0.07
Age	–	−0.01***
Female	–	−0.15***
BA degree or higher	–	0.38***
Supervisor position	–	0.01

Note: The table reports the coefficients from the hybrid (within–between) regression model. The dependent variable is AILRSE-5 (range 5–35, see Appendix). Both within-person and between-person effects are reported. Transformational leadership and social support are standardized. Age, gender, education, and supervisory position are time-invariant predictors and are therefore estimated at the between-person level only. Data used here involve *WorkAI* longitudinal data from 2025 (2 time points). The model includes 2746 observations from 1591 individuals. Statistical significance: *** $p < 0.001$, ** $p < 0.01$, * $p < 0.05$.

Table 5.5 Within- and between-person effects of AI learning readiness self-efficacy on specific forms of work-related AI use in Finland

Forms of work-AI use	*Within-person effects*	*Between-person effects*
Chatbots or virtual assistants	0.18**	0.38***
Machine learning for data analysis	0.08	0.19***
Natural language processing tools	0.08	0.17***
Robotic process automation	−0.03	0.09**
Image or video analysis tools	0.02	0.10**
Predictive analytics tools	0.01	0.09**
AI-enhanced decision support systems	0.06	0.08**
AI-enhanced customer relationship management	−0.02	0.13***
AI in cybersecurity tools	0	0.09**

Note: The table reports coefficients of AI learning readiness self-efficacy (AILRSE-5, see Appendix) from hybrid (within–between random-effects) panel regression models predicting the frequency of use of nine forms of work-related AI tools (measured in a range of 0–5). The AILRSE-5 is standardized (mean = 0, SD = 1). All models adjust for age, gender, education, and supervisory position. The models are based on three waves of *WorkAI* survey data from Finland in 2024 to 2025 (N = 2663 observations from 1357 individuals who have experience in using AI-related tools at work). Statistical significance levels: *** $p < 0.001$, ** $p < 0.01$, * $p < 0.05$.

self-efficacy is systematically related to different forms of AI use. At the between-person level, individuals with higher average self-efficacy reported more frequent use across nearly all AI tool categories, suggesting that those who perceive themselves as capable AI users are also more broadly engaged with AI in their work. At the within-person level, increases in self-efficacy over time were associated with increases in the use of chatbots and virtual assistants. The findings further confirm our earlier results that AI learning readiness self-efficacy is a central psychological resource underlying engagement with diverse AI applications at work.

Conclusion: Capability Over Exposure

An old saying suggests that "you can lead a horse to water, but you can't make it drink." The proverb describes a situation in which one can be offered help or resources but cannot be forced to accept them or act on them. It also captures the central insight of this chapter; providing access to new technology, training, or opportunity does not automatically translate into learning and engagement. Organizations may introduce tools that make workers' tasks easier or more efficient and offer guidelines and resources, yet whether workers adopt and take up these tools depends largely on their perceived capability and readiness to do so. Throughout this chapter, we have discussed and shown that self-efficacy plays a central role in AI use.

Workers who believe they can master AI tools are more likely to approach them with initiative. Our analyses showed that AI learning and readiness are associated with the use of multiple tools, indicating that readiness shows in broader experimentation and uptake. However, these user experiences and processes are also influenced by psychosocial factors. As the evidence from our data showed, higher frustration of competence needs is associated with lower perceived learning readiness self-efficacy toward AI. When basic psychological needs are thwarted, individuals may withdraw rather than explore, which can have a wider impact on work progress and personal development. However, SDT also suggests that unmet needs can motivate individuals to seek environments that can restore autonomy, competence, and relatedness. In the current context, this could mean that workers actively look for ways to regain control and autonomy, whether through training, experimenting, or peer support, when such resources are available.

Similar to the earlier chapters, we showed here that workers' internal processes in dealing with AI change do not unfold in isolation. This is also true for self-efficacy and willingness to learn. We show that social support and effective transformational leadership can enhance self-efficacy, potentially reinforcing confidence in trying, failing, and learning. This is crucial in helping workers who are appraising AI as intimidating or demanding and moving toward a more manageable challenge mindset. In this sense, self-efficacy is both an individual and a social asset. Sustaining self-efficacy and supporting the basic psychological needs of workers may be among the most critical focuses of intervention when ensuring that AI change supports workers' well-being and engagement.

Importantly, when self-efficacy is high and basic psychological needs are supported, workers are more likely to interpret AI as enabling. The analyses conducted in this chapter support the notion that the perceived gains from AI are a mechanism behind sustainable work engagement. These findings further suggest that the future worker could be defined as a capable worker with access to advanced tools and as someone who has the capacity to adapt, learn, and translate technological change into tangible gains. In the next chapter, we take a forward-looking perspective and reflect on what future workers may look like as AI becomes increasingly advanced and embedded in everyday work. Importantly, we examine what this shift implies for human creativity and agency and the emerging forms of human–AI interaction.

References

Bakker, A. B. (2011). An evidence-based model of work engagement. *Current Directions in Psychological Science, 20*(4), 265–269. https://doi.org/10.1177/0963721411414534

Bakker, A. B., Demerouti, E., & Sanz-Vergel, A. (2023). Job demands–resources theory: Ten years later. *Annual Review of Organizational Psychology and Organizational Behavior, 10*(1), 25–53. https://doi.org/10.1146/annurev-orgpsych-120920-053933

Bakker, A. B., Demerouti, E., & Sanz-Vergel, A. I. (2014). Burnout and work engagement: The JD–R approach. *Annual Review of Organizational Psychology and Organizational Behavior, 1*(2014), 389–411. https://doi.org/10.1146/annurev-orgpsych-031413-091235

Bakker, A. B., & Sanz-Vergel, A. I. (2013). Weekly work engagement and flourishing: The role of hindrance and challenge job demands. *Journal of Vocational Behavior, 83*(3), 397–409. https://doi.org/10.1016/j.jvb.2013.06.008

Bakker, A. B., Schaufeli, W. B., Leiter, M. P., & Taris, T. W. (2008). Work engagement: An emerging concept in occupational health psychology. *Work & Stress, 22*(3), 187–200. https://doi.org/10.1080/02678370802393649

Bandura, A. (1997). *Self-efficacy: The exercise of control.* W. H. Freeman and Company.

Bandura, A. (2023). Cultivate self-efficacy for personal and organizational effectiveness. In E. Locke & G. Pearce (Eds.), *Principles of organizational behavior: The handbook of evidence-Based management* (3rd ed., pp. 113–135). John Wiley & Sons. https://doi.org/10.1002/9781394320769.ch6

Bankins, S., Hu, X., & Yuan, Y. (2024). Artificial intelligence, workers, and future of work skills. *Current Opinion in Psychology, 58*, 101828. https://doi.org/10.1016/j.copsyc.2024.101828

Bartimote-Aufflick, K., Bridgeman, A., Walker, R., Sharma, M., & Smith, L. (2016). The study, evaluation, and improvement of university student self-efficacy. *Studies in Higher Education, 41*(11), 1918–1942. https://doi.org/10.1080/03075079.2014.999319

Bergdahl, J., Latikka, R., Celuch, M., Savolainen, I., Mantere, E. S., Savela, N., & Oksanen, A. (2023). Self-determination and attitudes toward artificial intelligence: Cross-national and longitudinal perspectives. *Telematics and Informatics, 82*, 102013. https://doi.org/10.1016/j.tele.2023.102013

Carless, S. A., Wearing, A. J., & Mann, L. (2000). A short measure of transformational leadership. *Journal of Business and Psychology, 14*(3), 389–405. https://doi.org/10.1023/A:1022991115523

Cheng, T., Zhang, P., Wen, Y., & Wang, L. (2020). Social media use and employee innovative performance: Work engagement as a mediator. *Social Behavior and Personality: An International Journal, 48*(1), 1–9. https://doi.org/10.2224/sbp.8698

Compeau, D., Gravill, J., Haggerty, N., & Kelley, H. (2015). Computer self-efficacy: A review. In P. Zhang & D. F. Galletta (Eds.), *Human-computer interaction and management information systems: Foundations* (pp. 239–275). Routledge.

Compeau, D. R., & Higgins, C. A. (1995). Computer self-efficacy: Development of a measure and initial test. *MIS Quarterly, 19*(2), 189–211. https://doi.org/10.2307/249688

Consiglio, C., Borgogni, L., Di Tecco, C., & Schaufeli, W. B. (2016). What makes employees engaged with their work? The role of self-efficacy and employee's perceptions of social context over time. *Career Development International, 21*(2), 125–143. https://doi.org/10.1108/CDI-03-2015-0045

Crawford, E. R., LePine, J. A., & Rich, B. L. (2010). Linking job demands and resources to employee engagement and burnout: A theoretical extension and meta-analytic test. *Journal of Applied Psychology, 95*(5), 834–848. https://doi.org/10.1037/a0019364

Deci, E. L., & Ryan, R. M. (2008). Self-determination theory: A macrotheory of human motivation, development, and health. *Canadian Psychology/Psychologie Canadienne, 49*(3), 182–185. https://doi.org/10.1037/a0012801

Demerouti, E., Bakker, A. B., Nachreiner, F., & Schaufeli, W. B. (2001). The job demands-resources model of burnout. *Journal of Applied Psychology, 86*(3), 499–512.

Demircioglu, M. A. (2018). Examining the effects of social media use on job satisfaction in the Australian public service: Testing self-determination theory. *Public Performance & Management Review, 41*(2), 300–327. https://doi.org/10.1080/15309576.2017.1400991

DiTommaso, E., Brannen, C., & Best, L. A. (2004). Measurement and validity characteristics of the short version of the social and emotional loneliness scale for adults. *Educational and Psychological Measurement, 64*(1), 99–119. https://doi.org/10.1177/0013164403258450

Eastin, M. S., & LaRose, R. (2000). Internet self-efficacy and the psychology of the digital divide. *Journal of Computer-Mediated Communication, 6*(1), JCMC611. https://doi.org/10.1111/j.1083-6101.2000.tb00110.x

Heiskari, M., Celuch, M., Koivula, A., Savolainen, I., & Oksanen, A. (2025). Technological identity and basic psychological needs in the use of new technologies: A two-wave cross-national survey study. *International Journal of Information Management, 84*, 102926. https://doi.org/10.1016/j.ijinfomgt.2025.102926

Kahn, W. A. (1990). Psychological conditions of personal engagement and disengagement at work. *Academy of Management Journal, 33*(4), 692–724. https://doi.org/10.5465/256287

Kaya, B., Çınar, S., & Cenkseven Önder, F. (2025). AI literacy and digital wellbeing: The multiple mediating roles of positive attitudes towards AI and satisfying basic psychological needs. *International Journal of Human–Computer Interaction, 42*, 1–11. https://doi.org/10.1080/10447318.2025.2499162

Kim, B. J., Kim, M. J., & Lee, J. (2024). The impact of an unstable job on mental health: The critical role of self-efficacy in artificial intelligence use. *Current Psychology, 43*(18), 16445–16462. https://doi.org/10.1007/s12144-023-05595-w

Kim, B. J., & Lee, J. (2024). The mental health implications of artificial intelligence adoption: The crucial role of self-efficacy. *Humanities and Social Sciences Communications, 11*(1), 1–15. https://doi.org/10.1057/s41599-024-04018-w

Kim, M., & Beehr, T. A. (2020). Thriving on demand: Challenging work results in employee flourishing through appraisals and resources. *International Journal of Stress Management, 27*(2), 111. https://doi.org/10.1037/str0000135

Knight, C., Patterson, M., & Dawson, J. (2017). Building work engagement: A systematic review and meta-analysis investigating the effectiveness of work engagement interventions. *Journal of Organizational Behavior, 38*(6), 792–812. https://doi.org/10.1002/job.2167

Latikka, R., Savela, N., & Oksanen, A. (2023). Perceptions of assistive robots at work: An experimental approach to social influence. *International Journal of Social Robotics, 15*(9), 1543–1555. https://doi.org/10.1007/s12369-023-01046-5

Latikka, R., Turja, T., & Oksanen, A. (2019). Self-efficacy and acceptance of robots. *Computers in Human Behavior, 93*, 157–163. https://doi.org/10.1016/j.chb.2018.12.017

Lesener, T., Gusy, B., Jochmann, A., & Wolter, C. (2020). The drivers of work engagement: A meta-analytic review of longitudinal evidence. *Work & Stress, 34*(3), 259–278. https://doi.org/10.1080/02678373.2019.1686440

Lesener, T., Gusy, B., & Wolter, C. (2019). The job demands-resources model: A meta-analytic review of longitudinal studies. *Work & Stress, 33*(1), 76–103. https://doi.org/10.1080/02678373.2018.1529065

Li, X., Seah, R. Y. T., & Yuen, K. F. (2025). Mental wellbeing in digital workplaces: The role of digital resources, technostress, and burnout. *Technology in Society, 81*, 102844. https://doi.org/10.1016/j.techsoc.2025.102844

Liang, M., Xin, Z., Yan, D. X., & Jianxiang, F. (2021). How to improve employee satisfaction and efficiency through different enterprise social media use. *Journal of Enterprise Information Management, 34*(3), 922–947. https://doi.org/10.1108/JEIM-10-2019-0321

Nagel, L. (2020). The influence of the COVID-19 pandemic on the digital transformation of work. *International Journal of Sociology and Social Policy, 40*(9–10), 861–875. https://doi.org/10.1108/IJSSP-07-2020-0323

Oksa, R., Kaakinen, M., Savela, N., Ellonen, N., & Oksanen, A. (2021). Professional social media usage: Work engagement perspective. *New Media & Society, 23*(8), 2303–2326. https://doi.org/10.1177/1461444820921938

Oksanen, A., Osma, T., Heiskari, M., Cvetkovic, A., Soares Ruokosuo, E., Koike, M., Arriaga, P., & Savolainen, I. (2026). Mapping AI learning readiness self-efficacy worldwide: Scale validation and cross-continental patterns. *Computers in Human Behavior: Artificial Humans, 7*, 100251. https://doi.org/10.1016/j.chbah.2026.100251

Poirier, C., & Gelin, M. (2025). Boosting workplace well-being: Unveiling the impact of digital tools. *Journal of Workplace Behavioral Health, 40*(4), 621–640. https://doi.org/10.1080/15555240.2024.2441209

Ranganathan, A., & Ye, X. M. (2026, February). AI doesn't reduce work—It intensifies it. *Harvard Business Review*. https://hbr.org/2026/02/ai-doesnt-reduce-work-it-intensifies-it

Ryan, R. M., & Deci, E. L. (2000). Self-determination theory and the facilitation of intrinsic motivation, social development, and well-being. *American Psychologist, 55*(1), 68. https://doi.org/10.1037/0003-066X.55.1.68

Ryan, R. M., & Deci, E. L. (2017). *Self-determination theory: Basic psychological needs in motivation, development, and wellness*. Guilford Publishing.

Savolainen, I., Ylinen, L., Grönroos, R., & Oksanen, A. (2026). AI transformation in working life: A systematic review of usage and attitudes towards AI among workers. *Digital Business, 6*(1), 100162. https://doi.org/10.1016/j.digbus.2025.100162

Schaufeli, W., & Bakker, B. A. (2013). Work engagement. In W. Ruch, A. B. Bakker, & L. Tay & F. Gander (Eds.), *Handbook of Positive Psychology Assessment* (pp. 273–295). Hogrefe.

Schaufeli, W. B., & Bakker, A. B. (2004). Job demands, job resources, and their relationship with burnout and engagement: A multi-sample study. *Journal of Organizational Behavior: The International Journal of Industrial, Occupational and Organizational Psychology and Behavior, 25*(3), 293–315. https://doi.org/10.1002/job.248

Schaufeli, W. B., Salanova, M., González-Romá, V., & Bakker, A. B. (2002). The measurement of engagement and burnout: A two sample confirmatory factor analytic approach. *Journal of Happiness Studies, 3*(1), 71–92. https://doi.org/10.1023/A:1015630930326

Schaufeli, W. B., Shimazu, A., Hakanen, J., Salanova, M., & De Witte, H. (2019). An ultra-short measure for work engagement. *European Journal of Psychological Assessment, 35*(4), 577–591. https://doi.org/10.1027/1015-5759/a000430

Schulz, C., Bendig, D., Bräunche, A., & Kindermann, B. (2026). Curse or blessing: Investigating the influence of firms' artificial intelligence adoption on employee job satisfaction. *Journal of Management Studies, 63*(2), 561–595. https://doi.org/10.1111/joms.70004

Seppälä, P., Mauno, S., Feldt, T., Hakanen, J., Kinnunen, U., Tolvanen, A., & Schaufeli, W. (2009). The construct validity of the Utrecht work engagement scale: Multisample and longitudinal evidence. *Journal of Happiness Studies, 10*(4), 459–481. https://doi.org/10.1007/s10902-008-9100-y

Sun, Y., Wu, L., & Jeyaraj, A. (2022). Moderating role of enterprise social media use in work engagement. *Information Processing and Management, 59*(1), 102793. https://doi.org/10.1016/j.ipm.2021.102793

Ulfert-Blank, A. S., & Schmidt, I. (2022). Assessing digital self-efficacy: Review and scale development. *Computers & Education, 191*, 104626. https://doi.org/10.1016/j.compedu.2022.104626

Vansteenkiste, M., Ryan, R. M., & Soenens, B. (2020). Basic psychological need theory: Advancements, critical themes, and future directions. *Motivation and Emotion, 44*(1), 1–31. https://doi.org/10.1007/s11031-019-09818-1

Vargo, D., Zhu, L., Benwell, B., & Yan, Z. (2021). Digital technology use during COVID-19 pandemic: A rapid review. *Human Behavior and Emerging Technologies, 3*(1), 13–24. https://doi.org/10.1002/hbe2.242

Wang, Y., Huang, Q., Davison, R. M., & Yang, F. (2021). Role stressors, job satisfaction, and employee creativity: The cross-level moderating role of social media use within teams. *Information & Management, 58*(3), 103317. https://doi.org/10.1016/j.im.2020.103317

Wang, Y. Y., & Chuang, Y. W. (2024). Artificial intelligence self-efficacy: Scale development and validation. *Education and Information Technologies, 29*(4), 4785–4808. https://doi.org/10.1007/s10639-023-12015-w

Ye, D., Xu, B., Wei, B., Zheng, L., & Wu, Y. J. (2024). Employee work engagement in the digital transformation of enterprises: A fuzzy-set qualitative comparative analysis. *Humanities and Social Sciences Communications, 11*(1), 1–15. https://doi.org/10.1057/s41599-023-02418-y

Zhang, J., Wu, X., Guo, J., & Jiang, R. (2022). The interactive effects of individual boundary spanning and boundary buffering when using enterprise social media. *International Journal of Information Management, 64*, 102490. https://doi.org/10.1016/j.ijinfomgt.2022.102490

Zhao, A. T., & Yu, Y. (2023). Employee online personal/professional boundary blurring and work engagement: Social media anxiety as a key contingency. *Computers in Human Behavior Reports, 9*, 100265. https://doi.org/10.1016/j.chbr.2022.100265

CHAPTER 6

The Future Worker: Rethinking Human Value

Abstract Artificial intelligence has long extended what humans can do creatively, but recent generative systems have begun to stretch the meaning of creativity, challenging traditional notions of authorship, skill, and innovation. As AI becomes embedded in everyday tasks, workers must navigate these shifting expectations and norms. Workers are, at the same time, required to adopt new tools (must), develop new competencies (know), build capability (can), and sustain intrinsic motivation (want). This chapter examines how these modalities influence and modify AI-driven transformation and the implications for the future of work and creativity. We explore how organizations can frame the direction and success of technological change. We also integrate perspectives on the social foundations of creativity and resilience, both of which are essential for successful transformation but depend on organizational contexts. The chapter argues that to realize the individual and collaborative creative potential of AI and human workers, obligation, capability, and motivation need to be aligned within supportive environments.

Keywords Artificial intelligence • Creativity • Agency • Innovation • Leadership • Organizations

A. Oksanen, I. Savolainen, *AI Disruption at Work*, Palgrave Advances in Work and Organizational Psychology,
https://doi.org/10.1007/978-3-032-35207-1_6

Creativity is at the core of what it means to be human. It has been associated with imagination, originality, and the capacity to transcend existing boundaries. Much cultural heritage is rooted in unique creativity, whether conducted in teams or as a solo effort. The history of world art is full of examples. Creativity was also something that AI research long considered to be the final frontier (Colton & Wiggins, 2012). It was widely assumed that AI would primarily automate routine cognitive tasks, leaving humans responsible for higher-order functions, such as empathy and creativity (Rust & Huang, 2021). However, these deeply rooted perceptions began to be challenged after 2022. Early examples of this development included artists winning art competitions with the use of AI. Famous cases include Jason M. Allen's use of the image generator Midjourney in a digital art competition in 2022 and Boris Eldagsen's 2023 victory at the Sony World Photography Awards with an AI-generated image. Both incidents sparked debate about the boundaries between human- and machine-produced art (Oksanen et al., 2023). After the initial shock, mostly stemming from the realization that AI-generated works could win in major competitions, the pace of AI development accelerated. For example, evidence based on research has consistently shown that people struggle to differentiate between man-made art and machine-made art (Bellaiche et al., 2023; Gangadharbatla, 2021; Oksanen et al., 2026).

Today's AI tools are increasingly sophisticated and often controversial in how they violate copyrights (Flick & Worrall, 2022; Oksanen et al., 2026; Piskopani et al., 2023). The practical consequence, however, is that even people working in cultural and creative industries are not protected from changes. Work that was once considered uniquely human is rapidly becoming subject to automation and machine-assisted production. The development of AI, especially in the creative sectors, forces us to reconsider human value. The rapid development of AI compels us to reconsider the value and meaning of human contributions. We argue that human creativity cannot be simply overcome, but with the presence of AI tools, there is an urgent need to re-examine what we mean by creativity and how we could update the discussion of creativity in the era of intelligent machines.

This chapter looks at the future of work and what remains uniquely human in the workplace in the age of AI. We discuss the role of human autonomy and human creativity by examining the evidence of computational creativity and experiments analyzing how people perceive AI-made art. We explore how creative intelligence becomes augmented through human–AI collaboration and what institutional, ethical, and leadership conditions are required to safeguard human value in increasingly automated environments. The chapter emphasizes that human value cannot be fully replaced by AI, although its significance may shift across different work contexts. Even in highly automated environments, human value can remain or become even more pronounced in the future workplace, as humans and AI must coexist, each contributing in distinct and complementary ways. We ground this work in theories of creativity adapted to the AI age. We also consider how AI could be used in the future so that we maintain the basic psychological needs of autonomy, competence, and relatedness that are central to human motivation and well-being.

Creative Intelligence and the Augmented Self

Creativity has been a central concept of modernity, emerging at least as early as the Renaissance, when individuality and the notion of the artist as a personality that transcends tradition, theory, and rules began to take shape (Hauser, 1977; Wolff, 1993). Artistic creativity has long been regarded as one of the highest expressions of human capability and identity. As such, it symbolizes the irreducible core of human uniqueness. Attempts to formalize and simulate creativity computationally have accompanied AI research since its early decades, becoming more systematic from the 1970s onward (Oksanen et al., 2023). One of the central figures in this area, Margaret Boden, discussed it in her book *Artificial Intelligence and Natural Man* (1977). Major developments in the field have been made, however, especially during the 2000s (Boden, 2010; Colton & Wiggins, 2012; Jordanous, 2016).

Google's DeepDream, released in 2015, is an early example of convolutional neural network-based software that was able to generate surreal, dream-like visuals. In the 2020s, GenAI tools—Stable Diffusion, Midjourney, and DALL-E for images, and Suno AI for music—shaped the possibilities for creative practices. OpenAI's Sora provides text-to-video solutions for some ChatGPT users. More recently, Seedance 2.0 by TikTok's developer, ByteDance, provided the next step by creating cinema-quality videos with music, sound effects, and dialogue with just a simple prompt. This put major Hollywood studios in alarm (Chia & Tewari, 2026). As we have seen before, the appeal of these tools stems from their ease of use. It is also worth noting that AI has been tested in the fine arts for years, across the visual arts, music, literature, performing arts, and architecture (Oksanen et al., 2023). Now, these creative options are, in essence, accessible to anyone, and creative gift or talent, whether innate or learned, is becoming less necessary. Not only is Hollywood shaking, but so is all business related to image, sound, and video.

Experimental evidence is piling up regarding whether humans can distinguish human-made art from AI-made art. Earlier experiments conducted at the turn of the 2020s showed that people struggled to differentiate between human-made and AI-generated artworks (Bellaiche et al., 2023; Gangadharbatla, 2021; Oksanen et al., 2026). More recent experiments have also shown that participants favored AI-made art over human-made art (van Hees et al., 2025). Experiments have also shown a bias against AI, meaning that humans value AI-made art aesthetically lower when they know its origin (Agudo et al., 2022; Bellaiche et al., 2023; Gangadharbatla, 2021; Horton Jr et al., 2023; Millet et al., 2023). Based on survey evidence, the use of AI in art raises concerns in people (Latikka et al., 2023; Oksanen & Lahtinen, 2026), but maybe less so than a couple of years ago. It is also likely that due to the development of AI tools and their popularity, people regard the use of AI in art more favorably (van Hees et al., 2025; Oksanen et al., 2026). This shift may extend more broadly across the cultural and creative industries. As AI-generated content floods digital environments, audiences may become more tolerant of machine-produced outputs. As a consequence, the expectation of human labor behind creative products might become less central for people.

As AI conquers fields that are dominated by humans only, it is worth asking whether AI can overcome human creativity completely. This is also a worrying question that is often present in daily debates. Joanna Zylinska states, *"What lies beneath current questions about machinic creativity is a deeper anxiety about the ways humans can continue to be creative, for how much longer, and at what cost"* (2023, p. 140). Understandably, these emerging changes complicate how creativity and creative value are understood. If audiences tend to value human-made products more highly, could this lead to a differentiation of categories in which a human-made artifact becomes more prestigious than an AI-assisted one? At the same time, AI tools may diversify culture and the creative industries by allowing the production of works such as music, literature, or art without prior experience or training. In this sense, many individuals may be able to pursue and achieve their creative goals through these means. Over time, this is likely to shift how creativity is understood. It may become less associated with skill and execution, and more with conceptual design and curation, whether the medium is a human mind or an AI tool. However, history has shown that new technologies do not usually diminish existing forms of creativity, as photography did not replace painting, and machine music did not replace acoustic instruments. Instead, they tend to expand the range of creativity. The possibilities this brings are yet to be discovered.

Boden (1998) makes an important distinction between combinational, exploratory, and transformational creativity. Combinational creativity simply reorders already existing elements, and novelty arises from unexpected juxtapositions. However, the conceptual framework does not change. This is the most common form of AI tools today. Exploratory creativity goes much further than this and considers new, undiscovered possibilities within an established framework. Transformational creativity is the rarest form of creativity and involves new ideas generated within a new conceptual framework. It takes a significant leap forward from a simple tweaking of what already exists. In other words, transformational creativity involves a paradigm shift. One example of this is the invention of perspective in Renaissance painting. Much of human-made art does not reach the level of transformational creativity. A totally different question is: Is it possible for AI to do so?

Teppo Felin and Matthias Holweg (2024) wrote an important article about why human cognition is fundamentally different from AI. Human cognition relies on theory-based causal reasoning, which is fundamentally forward-looking. AI instead utilizes probability-based knowledge. For example, large language models are trained with large data sets and could be considered imitation engines, or "stochastic parrots," but not linguistically innovative compared to even children. Felin and Holweg (2024) give a great example of an LLM set in the year 1633, when it would have had all the knowledge available back then. If asked about Galileo's heliocentric view, it would respond based on existing knowledge and reject Galileo's view. Regardless of how superior or advanced it is, or how large a data set it covers, past data cannot then fully compete with human cognition in its search for experimentation and novelty.

A recent meta-analysis by Holzner et al. (2025) investigated GenAI's performance on the basis of research results. GenAI alone matched human performance in creativity. However, humans utilizing AI outperformed humans working without such tools. A relevant third finding was that the use of AI had a negative effect on the diversity of ideas, which suggests that working with AI leads to more homogenous results (Holzner et al.,

2025). This is in line with what Felin and Holweg (2024) reported. AI is not a creative machine; it is a parroting machine. Hence, it may require skills from the users of GenAI to maintain a human creative mind and utilize AI as an assistant. The presence of AI tools is likely to affect the creative process. Zhou and Lee (2024) utilized data from 50,000 users and 4 million artworks to analyze the creative process. Users working with AI were more productive and doubled their creative artifacts. They also received better feedback. However, there was also a decrease in content novelty, which indicated a homogenization of artistic style. Despite this, the exploration of new ideas has increased. Zhou and Lee (2024) concluded that the greatest benefits of AI are gained by those who are able to capture novel ideas from a large number of provided possibilities. Individuals who excelled with novel ideas before the introduction of GenAI were especially able to gain the greatest benefits from it. Another study by Doshi and Hauser (2024) also discovered that, although stories written with AI were evaluated as better and more entertaining, they were also more alike.

We believe that the central question is not whether AI can be creative. The most important question is how humans remain creative and how they remain authors of their augmented creativity. AI is a potential tool, but a powerful servant is equally a dangerous master. The role of humans is decisive. AI augments human cognition at work. This argument, provided by the extended mind thesis, considers that cognitive processes are not confined to the brain but can extend into environmental and technological structures that function as components of cognitive systems (Clark & Chalmers, 1998; Farina & Levin, 2021). In contemporary digital environments, such extensions increasingly involve technological systems that augment human perception, memory, and problem-solving capacities (Raisamo et al., 2019). AI is simply a new form of technology that augments the self. In AI-mediated environments, workers increasingly operate as hybrid agents. Their imagination and decision-making are guided by algorithmic systems. This does not eliminate human agency but rather reconfigures it. A worker's self becomes relational, as creative acts emerge from interactive loops between human intention and machine suggestions. From the perspective of agency theory, such relationality is not new but is reconfigured. Emirbayer and Mische (1998) conceptualize agency as temporally embedded and based on past routines (iterational), imagining future possibilities (projective), and making situated judgments in the present (practical–evaluative). AI systems intervene in each of these dimensions. There is a fine balance between AI opening up creative possibilities and AI invading human thinking and homogenizing it.

What We Want, Know, Can, and Must Do in the AI Workplace

AI changes work, but creative minds are still needed in the workplace. What we saw earlier is that despite the remarkable capability of AI tools, the best outcome in different tasks is often gained when humans are in control and aim to maintain creative possibilities. There is always the danger that AI homogenizes options and limits out-of-the-box solutions. Hence, it is highly important to understand how workers maintain their creativity in the changing setting of work. Teresa M. Amabile's (1983a, 1983b, 1996) Componential Theory is one of the most influential theories of creativity. The original model emphasized intrinsic motivation and cognitive components, and later revisions (Amabile, 1996; Amabile & Pratt, 2016) incorporated contextual and organizational dynamics and framed creativity as a dynamic process embedded within social systems.

In *Creativity in Context* (1996), Amabile expanded her original theory and emphasized that creativity is an outcome of the interaction between individual abilities and the social environment. This model maintains three core components. The first component comprises the individual—domain-relevant skills. These refer to knowledge, skills, expertise, and the special talents demanded in certain domains. The second component is creativity-relevant processes. These involve cognitive abilities and personality traits that may involve, for example, risk taking and the capability to search for novel solutions. The third component is intrinsic motivation, which includes interest and internal drive. For example, in work settings, work engagement is the type of intrinsic motivation needed for creative solutions. Amabile (1996) considered these factors in a broader social context and discussed how organizational factors, such as autonomy, evaluation practices, time pressure, and leadership, influence these components. Componential Theory has been widely tested over decades. Amabile herself notes that the most important recent findings involve teams and organizations, where teams may benefit from individual skills, but also that teams can enhance individual-level creativity (Amabile & Pillemer, 2012).

What is remarkable about current AI tools is not only the ease of their use but also the creative possibilities they may allow. At the same time, it is almost too easy for a worker to rely strongly on AI and stop looking for optimal solutions and thinking in new ways. We consider creativity and work in the age of AI through a broader modal framework of human agency. Moving from psychological processes to modal structures that make action possible, we present a novel view of AI-assisted and augmented work using Greimas' theory. Algirdas Julien Greimas is a well-known French semiotician representing structural semiotics (Schleifer, 2017; Robichaud, 2002; Tarasti, 2017).

In his theory of modalities, Greimas (1986) identified four core modalities: *know* (*savoir*), *want* (*vouloir*), *can* (*pouvoir*), and *must* (*devoir*). The four modalities describe the conditions that structure action and must be in place for a subject to act. Savoir is knowledge or competence, indicating that the subject knows how to act; vouloir refers to wanting and corresponds to motivation; pouvoir refers to ability and being able, but could also be understood as possibility; and devoir describes having to, referring to necessity or obligation (Greimas & Courtés, 1982; Sulkunen & Törrönen, 1997). Modalities theory shifts attention from the structure of the object to the subject's competence and orientation toward it; in other words, to what the subject wants, knows, is able to do, or is obliged to do (Greimas & Courtés, 1982). This allows for the examination of the conditions for creativity, meaning, and action while still acknowledging the basic relationship between actor and task.

The idea of modalities also significantly expands the discussion of AI at work. It is not only about risks and opportunities, or demands and resources, but rather the complex relations that workers need to balance with one another. The introduction of new technologies may activate any of these modalities and be associated with experiences and emotions related to AI at work. For creativity, these modalities could be understood as qualifications of the subject; creativity depends not only on the production of an outcome (object) but also on whether the subject wants, knows, and is able to create within the newly given context. The modalities can also be situated within a broader narrative framework, drawing from Greimas' actantial model (Sulkunen & Törrönen, 1997). In this set-up, the worker can be understood as the subject of a narrative in search of, for instance, competence, security, or meaning in the face of technological change, which would be the valued objects. Their journeys may be influenced by supportive factors (e.g., tools, training programs, or colleagues) and opponents (e.g., opaque algorithms, managerial pressure, or lack of

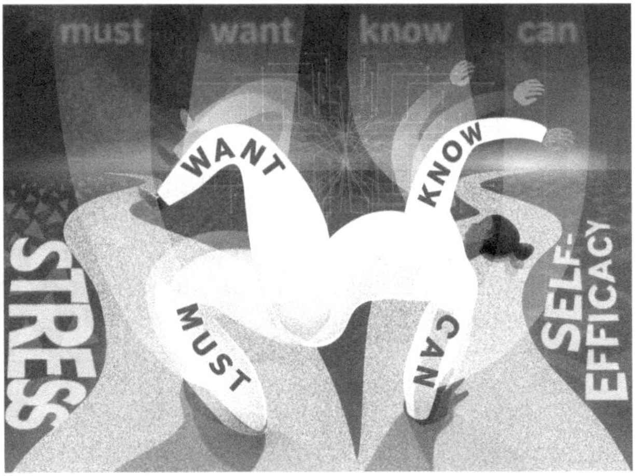

Fig. 6.1 Balancing between stress and self-efficacy. (Note: Picture by Ika Österblad, Mediakunta, Finland.)

institutional support). A semiotic perspective helps us to map how workers have to balance themselves in relation to the forces of change (see Fig. 6.1).

We interviewed 54 experts from six different organizations in Finland in the spring of 2024. Our interviews were conducted during the time when AI was increasingly coming to everyday practices, and it was the train that no one wished to miss, as one of our interviewees from IT services and consulting expressed: "*If you don't start using them and making them part of your role now, you might already be behind the curve*" (Participant 19). Another participant, an employee of a major Finnish city, expressed this similarly: "*Those who don't take it (AI) into use will unfortunately be left behind. That's maybe the most drastic bad thing about it*" (Participant 10).

The know (savoir) modality at work is associated with prior knowledge or competence in certain matters. Essentially, in working life, workers have their education, training, and extensive expertise to do the task they do. Most interviewees considered their capacity for work to have improved due to AI. It was considered a useful assistant, for example, in coding, analysis, and ideation. This is reflected in an interviewee's description of AI: "*If I were a pilot, AI would be a copilot and handle the more routine tasks during the flight. I could then focus on thinking about where we are flying and how*" (Participant 7, IT services and consulting). This positioning highlights that, while AI supports tasks, knowing is preserved in the human subject. AI has also displaced prior work, for example, in the IT sector, where human coding has been significantly replaced by AI modalities. These findings underline the role of AI in augmenting human tasks (Bankins et al., 2024; Fügener et al., 2026).

Want (vouloir) in this same context relates to workers' motivation and willingness to adopt AI. This is a crucial component of technology adoption because even if workers know how to use AI and are able to (can, pouvoir) use it, the action will not occur without willingness. In our sample, interviewees expressed interest in AI and held positive expectations about its ability to improve work practices in ways that matched their roles. The orientation toward wanting is illustrated in a comment by an interviewee from the forestry and paper industry: "*I am looking forward to how I could make use of it [AI] even better—where to find those gaps that fit in my own role, which I could fill with this AI*" (Participant 17), and another from IT services and consulting: "*But in reality, I have a keen interest in learning these things [AI], and I believe I can find my own niche—even if, at some point, AI could do what I currently do and consider as my role*" (Participant 14).

Within the modality of can (pouvoir), the element of being able to do or having the practical possibility of doing was emphasized. In the current AI adoption, a broader range of workers has been introduced to AI than previously. For many, opportunities to experiment with, learn, and use AI have primarily been enabled through their organizations. Some of our interviewees described having little prior familiarity with AI. For example, one participant stated, "*I am part of that generation; I am not, in that way, technology-oriented*" (Participant 38). At the same time, the role of employers in creating these opportunities was also experienced as beneficial. As one participant noted, "*We are a global business and, as such, invested in internal models... It helps in your personal work, so they encourage you to try AI*" (Participant 50, IT services and consulting).

All work includes elements that are a must. This devoir aspect comes through as very relevant in our findings. Mastering AI is considered a must. As one of our interviewees from the forestry and paper industry explained, "*It's clearly a skill you need to have. AI doesn't take jobs, but it does take them from those who don't know how to use it*" (Participant 36). Our interviewees perceived AI utilization as a critical factor for sustaining both individual and organizational competitiveness. The wish to learn and apply AI tools based on one's own interests and at one's own pace was not always realistic among workers in different roles and instead intensified their sense of obligation. One interviewee stated, "*There are people who are really enthusiastic about it… And if those people happen to be in managerial positions, then it might create, for me personally, a sort of need—driven more by necessity—to start using it*" (Participant 5, forestry and paper industry). Similar sentiments were raised by a participant from IT services and consulting: "*Well, I see it as an absolute requirement at this point, because these models are already good enough that you really can't afford not to use them*" (Participant 19).

Interviewees also recognized their responsibility as actors who will ultimately put AI into practice. This process is supported by factors such as organizations providing training or opportunities for peer learning. Such support appeared to ease appraisals: "*I don't see any panic about this. I think we've responded really well, and this is a good employer in that you're allowed and encouraged to train and learn—also in this area. That support is clearly visible even at the executive level*" (Participant 13, city organization/public administration). Simultaneously, interviewees described opposing factors and challenges, risks associated with the use of AI and stress related to the additional need to verify AI results. As one participant noted, "*You almost always have to admit that you're constantly a couple of steps behind this development. Because alongside work, you don't always have the time or energy to take on new things—like, 'I still have to study this, and I still have to study that'—and that kind of causes a bit of technostress*" (Participant 18, city organization/public administration). This is also aligned with our survey findings and other studies indicating that AI tools can introduce new cognitive and emotional demands (Chang et al., 2024).

In AI-mediated work environments, agency becomes increasingly relational and technologically situated. The theory of modalities clarifies the fundamental structure of action and considers what the subject wants, knows, can do, and must do (Greimas, 1986; Greimas & Courtés, 1982). As noted earlier, agency involves a temporal conception (Emirbayer & Mische, 1998; Saari et al., 2025), which is relevant for creativity as well. Work tasks require knowledge and expertise gained from iterations, but they have a significant future-looking element that is motivated by engagement and the desire to create. At the same time, creativity depends on what individuals are able to do in concrete situations and how they evaluate and solve emerging problems. The componential theory of creativity (Amabile, 1996; Amabile & Pratt, 2016) provides a psychological account of these capacities by specifying domain-relevant skills, creativity-relevant

Table 6.1 Modal, temporal, and psychological dimensions of agency and creativity in the AI workplace

Modality	*Agency dimension*	*Creativity component*	*Workplace meaning*
Know (savoir)	Iterational orientation	Domain-relevant skills	Expertise, knowledge base
Want (vouloir)	Projective orientation	Intrinsic motivation	Desire to create, autonomy, engagement
Can (pouvoir)	Practical-evaluative orientation	Creativity-relevant processes	Problem-solving ability
Must (devoir)	Structural conditioning of agency	Social/organizational environment	Norms, leadership, constraints

Note: The modal structure follows Greimas' (1986) theory of modalities. The temporal dimensions of agency are adapted from Emirbayer and Mische's (1998) conceptualization of iterational, projective, and practical-evaluative agency. The psychological components of creativity are based on Amabile's (1996) Componential Theory of Creativity.

processes, and motivation within organizational contexts. We consider these three (modalities, agency dimensions, and creativity components) to constitute how workers today are able to maintain their creativity and agency. Table 6.1 synthesizes these dimensions into a coherent analytical model of creative agency in the AI workplace. What is important is that these are based on the organizational context and situations. We consider that the future potential of human work requires organizational support and leadership that considers how humans can augment their abilities via AI but still remain future-looking, theory-building, and out-of-the-box thinkers.

Building a Space for Innovation

The future of work emerges through the contexts in which technologies are introduced, including organizational structures, everyday situations, and points of interaction between people and technology. We showed before that creativity and agency are context-dependent rather than individual traits. Amabile and Pratt (2016) emphasized that creativity in organizations is influenced by how work is designed, how resources are allocated, and how leaders create conditions that enable employees to develop and apply their expertise. We consider creativity to be the key to future human work. Many routine work tasks could be replaced by technology, but human orientation toward the future is something that is still needed in the age of AI. New technologies are not simply adopted; they are tools to be used. The future of human work involves creativity and the creation of new ideas and further innovations, which are the implementation of new ideas.

Well-being, engagement, and creativity at work are connected to organizational support, leadership, autonomy, and psychological safety, which allow workers to experiment and sometimes fail in their work tasks. Building a space for innovation requires more than adopting new technologies; it involves cultivating organizational environments that support autonomy, motivation, and experimentation. In previous chapters of this book, we have shown the importance of social support at workplaces from colleagues and supervisors. Social support protects workers from the feeling that their professional identities are threatened by AI (see Table 4.2 in Chap. 4). It is also widely connected to work engagement (see Table 5.1 in Chap. 5). Social support helps build an environment that enables creativity. This network of supportive colleagues, supervisors, and friends enables individuals to flourish. Essentially, a happy worker is an engaged worker, and engaged workers are more likely to see benefits in AI (see Table 5.2 in Chap. 5). These workers are also more likely to have high self-efficacy in learning new things with AI. These circumstances also allow creativity at work in the age of AI.

Leadership plays a central role in creating the conditions that enable flourishing work communities where there is room for creativity and the potential for innovations. Transformational leadership refers to leadership that seeks to inspire, motivate, and intellectually stimulate followers so that they transcend routine performance and pursue shared goals, innovation, and change (Bass, 1999; Bass & Riggio, 2006; Judge & Piccolo, 2004). In particular, it can provide vision, stimulation, and support that can provide a basis for both intrinsic motivation and psychological safety. We saw earlier in Chap. 5, for example, that transformational leadership was associated with AI learning readiness self-efficacy over time (see Table 5.4). It is then able to support an environment in which AI tools are experimented with. Transformational leadership often relies on the leader's charisma and idealized influence, through which they communicate vision and encourage followers to exceed their expectations. It is equally important to note that the positive and forward-driven aspects of transformational leadership could have a dark side and lead to worker exhaustion (Lin et al., 2019; Tourish, 2013).

Research on transformational leadership in AI-driven work environments is, at this point, limited. Findings on earlier technological changes, such as digitalized and virtual teams, offer useful insights into how leadership might support creative spaces in AI adoption. For instance, prior work has shown that the quality of written communication can predict transformational leadership in virtual teams, highlighting the importance of a leader's ability to convey vision and emotion in a new context through text-based interactions (Cortellazzo et al., 2019). Transformational leaders can also stimulate work engagement in remote settings, although their perceived digital communication skills play a moderating role in how leadership translates into engagement (Boccoli et al., 2024).

The change brought about by AI can be scary, and there is no way back from it now. Change is often inevitable in the workplace. Leadership scholar Rosabeth Moss Kanter (2009) wrote in her essay "To master change, first dread it" about the difficulty of change at work. People hate it fundamentally, and it can cause stress and loss of control. Change is disturbing and troubling, and to master it, one needs to encounter it and step out of one's comfort zone. In the best case, workers can engage with the change, and it becomes an opportunity. This captures a central dynamic in workplace AI transformation: technological change itself does not and cannot determine how it is experienced; rather, what matters is the workers' perspectives. Do they perceive themselves as passive recipients of change or active participants whose actions can meaningfully impact the change? For some workers, change may entail waiting to see what will happen to their roles and employment, whether their work will continue tomorrow. However, survival in working life transformation does not merely refer to retaining one's position but to adapting constructively and, ideally, growing to be better equipped than before.

Resilience is central to AI transformation. The concept itself refers to the ability to bounce back or sometimes forward after difficulties. Resilience was originally grounded in ecology and the natural sciences. Over the past several decades, it has become central in psychological work, describing a capacity involving flexibility, self-awareness, and helpful coping strategies (Bonanno, 2004; Fletcher & Sarkar, 2013; Southwick et al., 2014). Later, it has been utilized to understand how organizations, communities, and societies adapt, learn, and recover from crisis situations (Pinheiro et al., 2022; Ungar, 2018). A resilience perspective is also important in the analysis of technological transformation (Oksanen et al., 2021).

One of the key lessons from resilience research is that people are remarkably capable of recovering and adapting even to significant disruptions, especially when they perceive support, agency, and new opportunities (Bonanno et al., 2011, 2023; Fletcher & Sarkar, 2013; Friedberg & Malefakis, 2022). The emphasis on resilience is important in light of the broader cultural shift toward framing social and organizational challenges in psychological and emotional terms. Illouz (2007, 2008) argued that contemporary institutions increasingly translate structural and economic transformations into narratives of individual experience and emotional management. Also, in AI disruption, there is a tendency to talk only about people's personal ability to cope and adapt, although the change involves the whole organizational setting. A relational understanding of resilience therefore redirects attention from individual vulnerability to the structural and collective conditions that sustain agency and creativity.

The way change is introduced, supported, and framed can either strengthen or undermine workers' capacity to adapt (Liu et al., 2024; Trenerry et al., 2021). As Kanter (2009) suggested, workers who are involved in change are more likely to appraise it as an opportunity. In this sense, resilience becomes a precondition for reaching the next stage—the new space where innovation can happen. Without the capacity to cope, learn, and remain engaged, the longer-term benefits of transformation, such as new ways of innovating and forms of creativity, are less likely to be achieved. Although resilience and creativity are experienced at the individual level, they are influenced by the organizational environment. Creativity in organizations is a social process influenced by leadership, strategy, and policies, as well as coworkers' everyday interactions and team dynamics (Amabile & Pratt, 2016). Moreover, organizational progress can stimulate individual creativity, particularly when workers experience their work as meaningful and internalize the goals the organization sets for innovation. In AI transformation, this implies that resilience is supported when organizations provide a compelling rationale for change and enable workers to experience concrete progress in their work with AI.

Conclusion: A Room of One's Own?

Nearly a century ago, Virginia Woolf argued that in order to write fiction, a woman needed a room of her own (1929). This insight extends beyond the literature by suggesting that creativity requires more than talent; it requires enabling conditions. Today, in the age of AI, workers similarly need space. Beyond the physical, these are organizational, social, and psychological spaces in which workers can experiment, learn, and find meaning in their evolving roles. Resilience enables them to navigate through the uncertainty of transformation, but innovation flourishes only when organizations create the equivalent of a room of one's own for their workers. With the rapid pace of transformation, organizations can become preoccupied with acquiring updated tools, developing guidelines, and training. Amid this, it is important not to lose sight of the broader conditions under which human creativity and innovation can endure—namely, environments that provide autonomy, support, and a sense of purpose.

In many organizations, the future of work is currently being reconfigured by the balance among the four modalities: know, must, can, and want. Technological transformation often introduces a strong sense of must, with new tools to adopt, new competencies to acquire, and new expectations to meet. Yet, creativity, or sustainable change are rarely produced out of obligation alone. Knowledge, resources, and organizational support that enable people to experiment and engage with confidence are also required. Most critically, however, enduring transformation must involve intrinsic motivation—the desire to participate in creating not only new ways of working but new ideas and forms of creation. When organizations cultivate environments in which these modalities align, AI is less likely to be experienced as an imposed disruption and more as a space of possibility through which human agency and creativity continue to evolve.

References

Agudo, U., Arrese, M., Liberal, K. G., & Matute, H. (2022). Assessing emotion and sensitivity of AI artwork. *Frontiers in Psychology, 13*, 879088. https://doi.org/10.3389/fpsyg.2022.879088

Amabile, T. M. (1983a). *The social psychology of creativity*. Springer-Verlag.

Amabile, T. M. (1983b). The social psychology of creativity: A componential conceptualization. *Journal of Personality and Social Psychology, 45*(2), 357–376. https://doi.org/10.1037/0022-3514.45.2.357

Amabile, T. M. (1996). *Creativity in context*. Westview Press.

Amabile, T. M., & Pillemer, J. (2012). Perspectives on the social psychology of creativity. *The Journal of Creative Behavior, 46*(1), 3–15. https://doi.org/10.1002/jocb.001

Amabile, T. M., & Pratt, M. G. (2016). The dynamic componential model of creativity and innovation in organizations: Making progress, making meaning.

Research in Organizational Behavior, 36, 157–183. https://doi.org/10.1016/j.riob.2016.10.001

Bankins, S., Ocampo, A. C., Marrone, M., Restubog, S. L. D., & Woo, S. E. (2024). A multilevel review of artificial intelligence in organizations: Implications for organizational behavior research and practice. *Journal of Organizational Behavior, 45*(2), 159–182. https://doi.org/10.1002/job.2735

Bass, B. M. (1999). Two decades of research and development in transformational leadership. *European Journal of Work and Organizational Psychology, 8*(1), 9–32. https://doi.org/10.1080/135943299398410

Bass, B. M., & Riggio, R. E. (2006). *Transformational leadership*. Psychology Press.

Bellaiche, L., Shahi, R., Turpin, M. H., Ragnhildstveit, A., Sprockett, S., Barr, N., Christensen, A., & Seli, P. (2023). Humans versus AI: Whether and why we prefer human-created compared to AI-created artwork. *Cognitive Research: Principles and Implications, 8*(1), 42. https://doi.org/10.1186/s41235-023-00499-6

Boccoli, G., Gastaldi, L., & Corso, M. (2024). Transformational leadership and work engagement in remote work settings: The moderating role of the supervisor's digital communication skills. *Leadership & Organization Development Journal, 45*(7), 1240–1257. https://doi.org/10.1108/LODJ-09-2023-0490

Boden, M. (1977). *Artificial intelligence and natural man*. Basic Books.

Boden, M. A. (1998). Creativity and artificial intelligence. *Artificial Intelligence, 103*(1–2), 347–356. https://doi.org/10.1016/S0004-3702(98)00055-1

Boden, M. A. (2010). *Creativity and art: Three roads to surprise*. Oxford University Press.

Bonanno, G. A. (2004). Loss, trauma, and human resilience: Have we underestimated the human capacity to thrive after extremely aversive events? *American Psychologist, 59*(1), 20–28. https://doi.org/10.1037/0003-066X.59.1.20

Bonanno, G. A., Westphal, M., & Mancini, A. D. (2011). Resilience to loss and potential trauma. *Annual Review of Clinical Psychology, 7*(1), 511–535. https://doi.org/10.1146/annurev-clinpsy-032210-104526

Bonanno, G. A., Chen, S., & Galatzer-Levy, I. R. (2023). Resilience to potential trauma and adversity through regulatory flexibility. *Nature Reviews Psychology, 2*(11), 663–675. https://doi.org/10.1038/s44159-023-00233-5

Clark, A., & Chalmers, D. (1998). The extended mind. *Analysis, 58*(1), 7–19. http://www.jstor.org/stable/3328150

Chang, P. C., Zhang, W., Cai, Q., & Guo, H. (2024). Does AI-Driven technostress promote or hinder employees' artificial intelligence adoption intention? A moderated mediation model of affective reactions and technical self-efficacy. *Psychology Research and Behavior Management, 17*, 413–427. https://doi.org/10.2147/PRBM.S441444

Chia, O., & Tewari, S. (2026, February). The Chinese AI app sending Hollywood into a panic. *BBC News*. https://www.bbc.com/news/articles/ckg1dl410q9o

Colton, S., & Wiggins, G. A. (2012). Computational creativity: The final frontier? In L. De Raedt, C. Bessiere, D. Dubois, P. Doherty, P. Frasconi, F. Heintz, & P. Lucas (Eds.), *ECAI 2012: 20th European conference on artificial intelligence proceedings* (pp. 21–26). IOS Press. https://doi.org/10.3233/978-1-61499-098-7-21

Cortellazzo, L., Bruni, E., & Zampieri, R. (2019). The role of leadership in a digitalized world: A review. *Frontiers in Psychology, 10*, 456340. https://doi.org/10.3389/fpsyg.2019.01938

Doshi, A. R., & Hauser, O. P. (2024). Generative AI enhances individual creativity but reduces the collective diversity of novel content. *Science Advances, 10*(28), eadn5290. https://doi.org/10.1126/sciadv.adn5290

Emirbayer, M., & Mische, A. (1998). What is agency? *American Journal of Sociology, 103*(4), 962–1023. https://doi.org/10.1086/231294

Farina, M., & Levin, S. (2021). The extended mind thesis and its applications. In: M. D. Robinson & L.E. Thomas (Eds.), *Handbook of embodied psychology: Thinking, feeling, and acting* (pp. 127–147). Springer International Publishing. https://doi.org/10.1007/978-3-030-78471-3_6

Felin, T., & Holweg, M. (2024). Theory is all you need: AI, human cognition, and causal reasoning. *Strategy Science, 9*(4), 346–371. https://doi.org/10.1287/stsc.2024.0189

Flick, C., & Worrall, K. (2022). The ethics of creative AI. In C. Vear & F. Poltronieri (Eds.), *The language of creative AI: Practices, aesthetics and structures* (pp. 73–91). Springer. https://doi.org/10.1007/978-3-031-10960-7_5

Fletcher, D., & Sarkar, M. (2013). Psychological resilience: A review and critique of definitions, concepts, and theory. *European Psychologist, 18*(1), 12–23. https://doi.org/10.1027/1016-9040/a000124

Friedberg, A., & Malefakis, D. (2022). Resilience, trauma, and coping. *Psychodynamic Psychiatry, 50*(2), 382–409. https://doi.org/10.1521/pdps.2022.50.2.382

Fügener, A., Walzner, D. D., & Gupta, A. (2026). Roles of artificial intelligence in collaboration with humans: Automation, augmentation, and the future of work. *Management Science, 72*(1), 538–557. https://doi.org/10.1287/mnsc.2024.05684

Gangadharbatla, H. (2021). The role of AI attribution knowledge in the evaluation of artwork. *Empirical Studies of the Arts, 40*(2), 125–142. https://doi.org/10.1177/0276237421994697

Greimas, A. J. (1986). For a topological semiotics. In *The city and the sign: An introduction to urban semiotics* (pp. 25–54). Columbia University Press.

Greimas, A. J. & Courtés, J. (1982). *Semiotics and language: An analytical dictionary.* Indiana University Press.

Hauser, A. (1977). *The social history of art (Vol. 2): Renaissance, Mannerism, Baroque*. Routledge.

Herrman, H., Stewart, D. E., Diaz-Granados, N., Berger, E. L., Jackson, B., & Yuen, T. (2011). What is resilience? *The Canadian Journal of Psychiatry, 56*(5), 258–265. https://doi.org/10.1177/070674371105600504

Holzner, N., Maier, S., & Feuerriegel, S. (2025). Generative AI and creativity: A systematic literature review and meta-analysis. *arXiv preprint* https://arxiv.org/abs/2505.17241. https://doi.org/10.48550/arXiv.2505.17241

Horton, C. B., Jr., White, M. W., & Iyengar, S. S. (2023). Bias against AI art can enhance perceptions of human creativity. *Scientific Reports, 13*(1), 19001. https://doi.org/10.1038/s41598-023-45202-3

Illouz, E. (2007). *Cold intimacies: The making of emotional capitalism*. Polity Press.

Illouz, E. (2008). *Saving the modern soul: Therapy, emotions, and the culture of self-help*. University of California Press.

Jordanous, A. (2016). Four PPPPerspectives on computational creativity in theory and in practice. *Connection Science, 28*(2), 194–216. https://doi.org/10.1080/09540091.2016.1151860

Judge, T. A., & Piccolo, R. F. (2004). Transformational and transactional leadership: A meta-analytic test of their relative validity. *Journal of Applied Psychology, 89*(5), 755–768. https://doi.org/10.1037/0021-9010.89.5.755

Latikka, R., Bergdahl, J., Savela, N., & Oksanen, A. (2023). AI as an artist? A two-wave survey study on attitudes toward using artificial intelligence in art. *Poetics, 101*(December), 101839. https://doi.org/10.1016/j.poetic.2023.101839

Lin, S. H., Scott, B. A., & Matta, F. K. (2019). The dark side of transformational leader behaviors for leaders themselves: A conservation of resources perspective. *Academy of Management Journal, 62*(5), 1556–1582. https://doi.org/10.5465/amj.2016.1255

Liu, P., Zhang, F., Liu, Y., Liu, S., & Huo, C. (2024). Enabling or burdening?—The double-edged sword impact of digital transformation on employee resilience. *Computers in Human Behavior, 157*, 108220. https://doi.org/10.1016/j.chb.2024.108220

Kanter, R. M. (2009, August 5). To master change, first dread it. *Harvard Business Review*. https://hbr.org/2009/08/to-master-change-first-dread-i

Millet, K., Buehler, F., Du, G., & Kokkoris, M. D. (2023). Defending humankind: Anthropocentric bias in the appreciation of AI art. *Computers in Human Behavior, 143*, 107707. https://doi.org/10.1016/j.chb.2023.107707

Oksanen, A., Cvetkovic, A., Akin, N., Latikka, R., Bergdahl, J., Chen, Y., & Savela, N. (2023). Artificial intelligence in fine arts: A systematic review of empirical research. *Computers in Human Behavior: Artificial Humans, 1*(2), 100004. https://doi.org/10.1016/j.chbah.2023.100004

Oksanen, A., & Lahtinen, J. (2026). AI-generated art perception: A population study. *Leonardo*. https://doi.org/10.1162/LEON.a.2664.

Oksanen, A., Cvetkovic, A., & Savolainen, I. (2026). How AI transforms the world of the fine arts. In R. Ladhari (Ed.), *Encyclopedia of AI in marketing*. Springer. https://doi.org/10.1007/978-3-031-75316-9_81-1

Oksanen, A., Oksa, R., Savela, N., Mantere, E., Savolainen, I., & Kaakinen, M. (2021). COVID-19 crisis and digital stressors at work: A longitudinal study on the Finnish working population. *Computers in Human Behavior, 122*, 106853. https://doi.org/10.1016/j.chb.2021.106853

Pinheiro, M., Magalhães, E., & Baptista, J. (2022). Adolescents' resilience in residential care: A systematic review of factors related to healthy adaptation. *Child Indicators Research, 15*(3), 819–837. https://doi.org/10.1007/s12187-021-09883-4

Piskopani, A. M., Chamberlain, A., & Ten Holter, C. (2023). Responsible AI and the arts: The ethical and legal implications of AI in the arts and creative industries. In *TAS '23: Proceedings of the First International Symposium on Trustworthy Autonomous Systems*, 48, 1–5. https://doi.org/10.1145/3597512.3597528.

Raisamo, R., Rakkolainen, I., Majaranta, P., Salminen, K., Rantala, J., & Farooq, A. (2019). Human augmentation: Past, present and future. *International Journal of Human-Computer Studies, 131*, 131–143. https://doi.org/10.1016/j.ijhcs.2019.05.008

Robichaud, D. (2002). Greimas' semiotics and the analysis of organisational action. In K. Liu, R. J. Clarke, P. B. Andersen, & R. K. Stamper (Eds.), *Coordination and communication using signs: Studies in organisational semiotics* (pp. 129–149). Springer US. https://doi.org/10.1007/978-1-4615-0803-8_6

Rust, R. T., & Huang, M. H. (2021). The feeling economy. In *The feeling economy: How artificial intelligence is creating the era of empathy* (pp. 41–61). Springer International Publishing. https://doi.org/10.1007/978-3-030-52977-2_4

Saari, E., Koskela, I., & Känsälä, M. (2025). Temporal orientations in human agency: A case of homecare practitioners as mobile phone users. *Information Technology & People, 38*(8), 1–18. https://doi.org/10.1108/ITP-12-2023-1291

Schleifer, R. (2017). *A. J. Greimas and the nature of meaning: Linguistics, semiotics and discourse theory*. Routledge.

Southwick, S. M., Bonanno, G. A., Masten, A. S., Panter-Brick, C., & Yehuda, R. (2014). Resilience definitions, theory, and challenges: Interdisciplinary perspectives. *European Journal of Psychotraumatology, 5*(1), 25338. https://doi.org/10.3402/ejpt.v5.25338

Sulkunen, P., & Törrönen, J. (1997). The production of values: The concept of modality in textual discourse analysis. *Semiotica, 113*(1/2), 43–69.

Tarasti, E. (2017). The semiotics of A. J. Greimas: A European intellectual heritage seen from the inside and the outside. *Sign Systems Studies, 45*(1–2), 33–53.

Tourish, D. (2013). *The dark side of transformational leadership: A critical perspective*. Routledge.

Trenerry, B., Chng, S., Wang, Y., Suhaila, Z. S., Lim, S. S., Lu, H. Y., & Oh, P. H. (2021). Preparing workplaces for digital transformation: An integrative review and framework of multi-level factors. *Frontiers in Psychology, 12*, 620766. https://doi.org/10.3389/fpsyg.2021.620766

Ungar, M. (2018). Systemic resilience: principles and processes for a science of change in contexts of adversity. *Ecology and Society, 23*(4), 34. https://doi.org/10.5751/ES-10385-230434

van Hees, J., Grootswagers, T., Quek, G. L., & Varlet, M. (2025). Human perception of art in the age of artificial intelligence. *Frontiers in Psychology, 15*, 1497469. https://doi.org/10.3389/fpsyg.2024.1497469

Wolff, J. (1993). The social production of art. In *The social production of art* (pp. 26–48). Macmillan Education UK. https://doi.org/10.1007/978-1-349-16517-9_3

Woolf, V. (1989). *A room of one's own*. HarperCollins. (Original work published 1929).

Zhou, E., & Lee, D. (2024). Generative artificial intelligence, human creativity, and art. *PNAS Nexus, 3*(3), pgae052. https://doi.org/10.1093/pnasnexus/pgae052

Zylinska, J. (2023). Art in the age of artificial intelligence. *Science, 381*(6654), 139–140. https://doi.org/10.1126/science.adh0575

CHAPTER 7

Imagining a Human-Centered AI Future

Abstract In this final chapter, we bring together the core insights of this book, reflecting on how AI is transforming workplaces, workers, and societies. Drawing on themes developed throughout the book, we outline key implications and future directions for research, practice, and policy. The chapter considers both current developments and possible future trajectories, highlighting the importance of human-centered approaches at work, leadership, resilience, and supportive organizational environments. We further examine the ethical implications of AI-driven change and the global inequalities that impact AI preparedness and access to its benefits. We conclude by outlining a road map toward a globally sustainable working life in the age of AI, aligning technological advancement with human thriving, creativity, and inclusive economic development.

Keywords Artificial intelligence • Work • Ethics • Sustainability • Resilience

AI transforms ways of working and the work conditions under which human agency and meanings are enacted. AI is essentially everywhere, and different AI solutions have been integrated into tools that people have used for years, from search engines to word processors. AI agents function at an increasingly high level, and they autonomously perform work tasks, assist in

A. Oksanen, I. Savolainen, *AI Disruption at Work*, Palgrave Advances in Work and Organizational Psychology,
https://doi.org/10.1007/978-3-032-35207-1_7

decision-making, and augment human productivity. Recent developments in agentic AI further extend these capabilities by enabling coordinated systems of agents to execute complex workflows and tasks (Sapkota et al., 2026). Artificial general intelligence (AGI) has developed from a theoretical idea to a potential, relatively near-future objective (Sarikaya, 2025). These developments, which were previously concentrated in specialized domains, are now reshaping expectations across entire labor markets.

Amid this change, it is important to take a step back and ask what this fundamentally means for workers and work itself. Our book has underlined the human perspective. AI is not merely another office tool; it is reshaping how people work both in offices and at home. More than that, AI has a major impact that is already visible in other working sectors as well, including the service sector and industry. An illustrative example of AI entering the service sector is Burger King's use of AI-based systems to monitor employees' interactions with customers and assess service quality (Roth, 2026). We believe that there is simply no sector in working life that has not been impacted by AI technologies. Although the use of AI tools at work is still more common among highly educated workers, the applications are wide-ranging and increasingly relevant, well beyond traditionally high-skill roles. Workers must negotiate their autonomy, identity, and competence in environments that are increasingly mediated and governed by algorithmic systems.

We have shown that AI is a potential stress factor for employees, making supportive measures in work organizations important. Workers with higher work engagement are the ones who are most likely to benefit from AI tools. According to our results, work engagement and self-efficacy were key to understanding the psychological side of AI adoption. We further showed that positive forward-driven leadership and support from colleagues were crucial. Our evidence shows that the direction and nature of the future of work is not determined by technology alone. Rather, it is influenced by the organizational, social, and political choices that govern how AI is designed, implemented, and distributed. A human-centered AI future requires more than technical optimization. Ethical reflection is highly important in determining what kind of work we value, how we treat workers, and how opportunities and risks are shared across societies.

This final chapter of our book synthesizes the psychological, organizational, and societal lessons of the preceding chapters and situates them within a broader ethical framework. The future of work is ethically contingent and shaped by responsibilities enacted within organizations, negotiated in societies, and embedded in global economic structures. We provide theoretical and practical implications for workplaces and policies. The ongoing AI disruption requires us to ask how to best prioritize long-term human flourishing over short-term efficiency. Imagining a human-centered AI future requires both critical and constructive imagination—how to put humans first and consider sustainable working life globally. This involves cultivating resilience without individualizing structural pressures. Innovations should lead to shared prosperity rather than deepening inequality. We provide a road map for ethically sustainable and resilient work in this chapter.

Workplaces in Motion

Disruption does not necessarily entail rupture. Although AI is likely to take over some work tasks and profoundly change ways of working, organizations have the unique opportunity to consider how work is organized (Savolainen et al., 2026). Ethics are at the core of AI discussions today. The key ethical principles of the *AI4People* framework consider beneficence and nonmaleficence, autonomy, justice, and explicability (Floridi et al., 2018). Thus, AI should promote human well-being and dignity (beneficence) and prevent harm (nonmaleficence). Both the risks and benefits of AI should be distributed fairly (justice), and AI systems should be transparent, intelligible, and accountable (explicability). Regulatory initiatives such as the EU AI Act translate several of these ethical principles into binding legal requirements (Buttaboni & Floridi, 2026). However, at the global level, AI development remains fragmented, with significant variation in how ethical safeguards are defined, implemented, and enforced.

Bankins and Formosa (2023) integrated the *AI4People* framework into their discussion of meaningful human work in the AI era. According to them, the five dimensions of meaningful work are task integrity, skill cultivation, task significance, autonomy, and belongingness. AI can weaken or strengthen these. AI can augment human capabilities and free up time previously spent on essential but laborious tasks. Consequently, it can have a positive effect on skill development and autonomy. The risks are related to AI fragmenting work into monitoring tasks, increasing surveillance, and replacing tasks that would require complex human judgment. These dimensions have a generally good fit with our perspectives and the results we have shown. Based on Self-determination Theory (Deci & Ryan, 2000), we showed the relevance of the human experience of autonomy and competence in AI adoption and use. Moreover, our results showed the relevance of relatedness, social support, and social belonging in meaningful social interactions, which supported the well-being of workers during transition. These findings are also backed up by previous research and evidence on self-determination theory in the contexts of technology use (Heiskari et al., 2025; Latikka et al., 2026) and work (Coxen et al., 2021; Van den Broeck et al., 2016).

Our results have major theoretical implications, fill existing gaps in the emerging literature on AI's impact on workplaces (Savolainen et al., 2026), and inform future studies aiming to understand AI's evolving role in workplaces. First, we demonstrated the centrality of social and professional identities in the adoption of AI. Humans are inherently social beings, and the formation of self and personal identity is shaped by relationships with others (Baumeister, 2022). AI adoption is a group behavior that takes place within teams and organizational contexts. We showed that if people identify strongly with other new technology users, they tend to hold more positive attitudes toward AI and are more likely to utilize it themselves. This indicates that if technology use is a central part of workers' identities, workers are more likely to have a positive approach to the technology in question. We also demonstrated the relevance of professional identity. We showed that AI can significantly threaten workers' professional identities, which is typically an unpleasant experience and contributes to stress. These results extend previous analyses concerning the topic (Mirbabaie et al., 2022). Integrating AI use safely into parts of personal and professional identities is likely to promote a more positive approach to AI among workers.

The second major theoretical implication is the central role of self-efficacy in learning and adopting new AI tools. According to our findings, AI learning readiness self-efficacy systematically explains the use of AI tools at work. These findings extend recent scholarship on the topic (Oksanen et al., 2026). Self-efficacy functions as a resource in work and is associated with positive AI attitudes and social identity as a new technology user. Longitudinal findings from Finland further showed that AI learning readiness self-efficacy was associated with the use of various AI solutions at work. Moreover, our findings suggest that transformational leadership increases AI learning readiness self-efficacy at work. This is important considering that organizational support for workers during AI disruption is a significant resource and facilitator of positive outcomes, both in terms of worker well-being and successful uptake. We consider that this type of organizational support is crucial, as AI is not simply another digital tool at the office. When it comes to AI, what matters far more than mere use is how workers use these tools. Our empirical research also showed that engaged workers appraised AI tools as useful for them and saw many benefits associated with their use. Our evidence suggests that appropriately integrated AI use can enhance employee well-being, particularly among engaged workers with high AI learning readiness self-efficacy.

Our third major theoretical implication is the role of creativity in work. Because AI is expected to reshape some work tasks and take over others, even tasks requiring empathy and social intelligence may be impacted, but creativity is potentially the human factor that is going to be difficult for AI to replace. Humans, at their best, think outside the box and find new and unexpected solutions to problems. In essence, they are forward-thinking (Felin & Holweg, 2024). Humans are uniquely capable of imagining how the world might be otherwise. As philosopher Hannah Arendt (1998) reminds us, through action, we bring new realities into being rather than simply adapting to existing ones. Our agency is based on projective orientation (Emirbayer & Mische, 1998). Creativity at work is a dynamic phenomenon involving teamwork that significantly benefits from people's individual strengths (Amabile & Pratt, 2016). This creativity can be amplified by good management and leadership.

From a practical perspective, our findings highlight that supporting workers' well-being during the AI disruption is an ethical responsibility but, equally importantly, a productivity and innovation issue. When workers are mentally and physically well, they are more likely to remain engaged, learn new tools, and contribute creatively. Conversely, if AI adoption reduces workers' autonomy or undermines the perceived meaning of their work, work engagement may decline and stress may increase. Such experiences can translate into lower work quality and reduced productivity. While these costs are borne by employers through weaker performance and potential loss of personnel, they may also extend more broadly to society through reduced labor market participation, slower economic growth, and weakened competitiveness. Consequently, health, education, and social support services may experience increased pressure because workers experience greater mental health strain, the demand for reskilling grows, and the need for social protection is higher.

At the same time, the findings presented here point to significant positive implications if organizations carefully consider these dynamics. Supporting work engagement, self-efficacy, and resilience through visible processes and psychologically safe environments can help maintain worker well-being and innovation capacity in the long term. Organizations that foster a supportive working climate and frame AI as augmentation rather than replacement may see more effective skill development and improved organizational agility. In any organizational change, successful implementation requires mutually supportive efforts from both leadership and employees, combining top-down and bottom-up involvement (Heyden et al., 2017). When those affected by the change are meaningfully involved, the change is more likely to become part of the organizational culture and produce positive outcomes. In the current AI transition, organizations and workers alike stand before something genuinely new. Although the change is brought about by technology, people drive its direction and consequences. Thus, the most effective transition must remain human-centered by design.

Societies in Transition

The transformation driven by AI is bringing immediate consequences for working life with many effects already visible. AI tools are enhancing productivity, reducing repetitive tasks, allowing creative experimentation, and expanding access to specialized knowledge. Tools are increasingly integrated into existing digital systems and facilitate, for example, AI-augmented collaboration and the automation of workflows with AI agents. The development of both software and hardware is currently rapid, and major technology companies have made substantial investments and introduced regular updates to their products. In this situation, disruption and hype go hand in hand, and both the positive and negative aspects of AI development are widely discussed societally. An interesting media study on over 10,000 AI and automation articles published in 1985–2020 in *The New York Times* and *The Washington Post* shows a shift from dystopian anxiety toward benefit-oriented narratives. Ethical and work-related concerns remain central and ambivalent over time (Cools et al., 2024). However, the emphasis on risks related to AI was strengthened in the 2020s. Overall, AI development is a vast field, and the voices most often heard are those of the leaders of tech companies. A common factor between critics and optimists is that they mostly agree that change is inevitable.

Global institutional actors, such as the World Economic Forum (2025), frame artificial intelligence primarily as a catalyst for large-scale job transformation and skill renewal. They emphasize adaptation and reskilling as essential strategies for responding to current changes. However, these reports are based on surveys of employers and reflect their expectations rather than changes in the job market. Empirical evidence suggests a more uneven and temporally layered process. A study based on a time-series analysis of Google search trends suggests short-term labor market deterioration followed by longer-term improvements aligned with productivity gains (Yilmazkuday, 2025). If some jobs do not completely disappear, they will at least change permanently. There is also a risk of further exacerbating job precarity, but it is too early to determine its extent. Evidence from the United States indicates that early-career workers are particularly likely to experience a decline in employment (Brynjolfsson et al., 2025a). Similar findings have not yet been consistently confirmed in other countries, although the evidence base is still emerging and may vary across institutional and labor market contexts (Goller et al., 2025; Kauhanen & Rouvinen, 2026).

Recent evidence suggests that less-experienced or lower-skilled workers benefit more from GenAI in well-structured tasks. In more complex settings, outcomes depend more strongly on domain expertise and the ability to critically evaluate AI outputs (del Rio-Chanona et al., 2025). Younger generations are more willing to utilize AI, but simple engagement with new technologies is not enough. The manner in which they are used is more decisive. Moreover, there is strong evidence showing the relevance of education. A recent paper by Cazzaniga et al. (2025) analyzing the United Kingdom and Brazil shows that young college-educated workers are more likely to benefit from AI exposure, whereas low-educated workers face higher risks of displacement. Young individuals with higher education appear more capable of transitioning from occupations negatively affected by AI to AI-complementary occupations. These results align with our discussion of the human role in changing situations. We think that the ability to move into new roles is crucial. Psychological factors, education, and other sociodemographic characteristics shape individuals' willingness and capacity to pursue such transitions.

Looking ahead, Restrepo (2025) considers the forthcoming AGI and warns that inequality may increase. Those whose work cannot be fully automated benefit from the situation, but there is a risk of a decline in wages, among others. In other words, structurally, we are not merely talking about recomposing tasks but rather intensifying labor market inequalities. We are currently in a decisive moment when societal preparation for AI needs to be taken seriously. Public discussions about AI often emphasize the potential productivity gains from these technologies without fully considering their long-term sustainability. Meaningful human work in the future necessitates AI governance that acknowledges dignity and fairness. Moreover, societal policies that enable inclusive skill and labor transitions are needed. Societal resilience in the age of AI requires considering job replacement and societal costs. Globally, this is an even more complex situation due to major differences in technological capacity, financial resources, and welfare systems. Acemoglu (2025a) argues that the future of AI is fundamentally political: Without multipolar governance that includes worker voices and developing nations, AI reinforces inequality and concentrates power and benefits.

As the current AI transformation continues to unfold, its long-term implications for work and society remain uncertain. Research on digital inequality has traditionally been framed through the concept of digital divides, which emphasize differences in access to, skills in using, and outcomes from digital technologies (van Dijk, 2020). Research on digital divides in the AI era confirms earlier findings regarding digital skills, socioeconomic resources, and organizational capabilities (Muhammad et al., 2025; Suárez & García-Mariñoso, 2025). Emerging evidence, however, shows that the AI digital divide is a complex and layered phenomenon. The diffusion of AI technologies may reinforce existing digital divides and introduce new dimensions of inequality in access, capabilities, and outcomes. Table 7.1 summarizes the key dimensions of AI-related digital divides and the mechanisms through which they shape inequalities in the adoption and outcomes of AI technologies.

Inequalities often arise first in access to technologies and lack of supportive infrastructure. Even though many AI tools are publicly available, meaningful use often depends on organizational licenses, integration into work systems, and the type of information accessed. Subsequently, the access gap is not just an individual issue; it varies across organizations, sectors, and regions (Acemoglu, 2025a). This suggests that access to AI is institutionally mediated, determining which workers can use it and under what conditions it is used. However, inequalities still arise even when access exists due to differences in AI-related capabilities. For instance, recent studies on algorithmic literacy show that awareness and understanding of AI technologies vary significantly across sociodemographic groups, potentially leading to a new algorithmic divide (Haider et al., 2026). Our own results showed the high relevance of self-efficacy in learning and adopting AI (see Chap. 5; Oksanen et al., 2026).

Table 7.1 Key digital divides in AI disruption

AI divide	*Key Question*	*Mechanisms*
Access divide	Who has access to AI tools and digital infrastructure?	Availability of AI systems, internet connectivity, computing resources
Capability divide	Who has the skills to effectively use AI technologies?	AI learning readiness self-efficacy, AI literacy, education level, generational differences
Task exposure divide	Which occupations are more exposed to AI technologies?	Differences in task composition (cognitive vs. manual tasks, knowledge-intensive work)
Returns divide	Who benefits from the economic advantages generated by AI?	Wage premiums, productivity gains, firm profits
Institutional divide	How do institutional environments shape AI adoption and outcomes?	Regulation, education systems, labor market institutions

The impact of AI also depends on task exposure—that is, the extent to which the tasks embedded in particular jobs can be augmented or automated by AI. Recent work highlights that AI's transformative power operates mainly through the alteration of specific work tasks, implying that workers' opportunities to benefit from AI will vary with the task content of their roles (Restrepo, 2025). All these differences may eventually translate into a returns divide, in which productivity gains, wage growth, or career advancement associated with AI adoption are disproportionately spread across certain workers, depending on skill, experience, and task context (Brynjolfsson et al., 2025b; Noy & Zhang, 2023). At this point, we can only make informed speculations about what the future will look like in terms of work and society and whether outlooks are pessimistic or optimistic (Cools et al., 2024). Nevertheless, what is inevitable is that AI will have profound implications for the trajectories of work and economic development. Experts, such as Nobel Prize–winner Daron Acemoğlu (2025b), consider that AI is likely to increase rather than reduce inequality. The likelihood of relying only on machine labor increases with AGI (Restrepo, 2025). AI may also impact democratic institutions and civic participation, as AI-driven information systems could have the potential to improve access to reliable information, enhance transparency, and create new possibilities for citizen participation in decision-making (Acemoglu, 2025a). Governments around the world are increasingly responding to AI's system-wide implications and economic potential through regulation, investment, and institutional development. According to the Stanford Institute for Human-Centered Artificial Intelligence (2025), legislative mentions of AI have risen by 21% across 75 countries since 2023, reflecting growing global policy attention. However, the scale and speed of these efforts differ significantly between countries, revealing uneven levels of preparedness and readiness. These differences are likely to influence how AI-mediated labor markets develop. Some scholars have warned that AI systems often rely on extensive amounts of hidden human labor. Different forms of ghost work and microwork are performed through digital platforms by geographically dispersed workers, typically situated in the Global South, as technology companies search for the most cost-effective sources of labor (Gray & Suri, 2019; Muldoon et al., 2024; Tubaro et al., 2020). As AI technologies continue to expand, these arrangements may grow together with more visible forms of short-term and gig work, creating opportunities for flexible participation but also raising new concerns about income stability, labor protection, and global inequality (Cedefop, 2025). Governments' responses to these challenges will determine whether AI labor markets reduce or reinforce existing and emerging divides.

A Road Map for a Globally Sustainable Work Life

AI development can be compared to environmental change, in that both represent rapidly evolving global challenges that require societal responses. In both fields, a growing body of research suggests that current trajectories are likely to produce problematic outcomes. Efforts to regulate them are particularly challenging when policy responses are uneven across regions of the world (Acemoglu, 2025a). Attempts to establish common governance frameworks often seek to reconcile the interests of regulators, industry actors, and ethical experts through shared concepts such as trustworthy AI (Stamboliev & Christiaens, 2025). Currently, when it comes to AI development, the public discussion is often dominated by promises coming from the technology industry itself.

Societally, AI development could bring major increases in inequality (Acemoglu, 2025b; Restrepo, 2025) and further evolve the current disruption into rupture. All of this is avoidable, and there are means to cope with the ongoing change. Research on economic progress has shown that increases in productivity or economic output do not necessarily translate into lasting improvements in human well-being or societal outcomes (Sarracino & O'Connor, 2021). The same message should be taken into account in AI development and integration. AI development should involve a strong emphasis on ethics (Floridi et al., 2018), while integration should be considered from the perspectives of meaningful work (Bankins & Formosa, 2023), human well-being, and social values. In the long term, technology development should not function solely as a source of profit for a privileged few across the globe.

Our approach in this book places human workers at the center of technological transformation. We argue that AI can be used to improve working life and promote the common good at both the societal and global levels. In this spirit, the concept of Industry 5.0 has recently been proposed to describe a new phase of industrial transformation that emphasizes human-centric innovation, sustainability, and the integration of advanced technologies with meaningful human work (Adel, 2022; Czvetkó et al., 2025; Li & Duan, 2025). The lessons from our book and findings point to several opportunities that are feasible at the grassroots level. We should not interpret the ongoing AI transformation as a deterministic process. AI transformation is an opportunity to consider novel innovations, possibilities for human creativity, and outside-the-box solutions that are not governed by tech conglomerates. The road ahead may follow bifurcating paths, echoing Jorge Luis Borges' (1964) metaphor of a garden of forking paths, in which different choices may lead to very different technological and societal futures.

Our road map of ethical and resilient working life in the age of AI (see Fig 7.1) is grounded in a fair global system and responsible societies. The figure illustrates the steps involved in workplace transformation. A just global system forms the broader foundation, while responsible societies provide the institutional structures that support these workplace transformations. Our first step is *human agency*, which should be considered a starting point when designing AI solutions for workplaces. AI should augment human capabilities, not replace human work. This leads to the second step: *meaningful work*. Ultimately, work without meaning is not only risky but also expensive for work organizations. Organizations should consider how AI tools help workers focus on meaningful work tasks. This is important, for example, when considering the use of AI agents, where the human role should not be reduced to the role of a supervisor. *Capability* is directly related to meaningful work. Self-efficacy in learning and adopting AI tools is highly important during AI disruption. Capability building is directly associated with well-being at work, and organizations should facilitate this for their workers.

The next step is *participation*, which involves strengthening worker involvement. Workers should be actively involved in decision-making

Fig. 7.1 Road map for an ethical and resilient working life in the age of AI

processes, ensuring that those most affected by technological change have a voice in influencing how technology is implemented and used. Next, organizations should embed *ethical* reflection in AI development and deployment. Today, the AI landscape is largely dominated by major technology companies primarily based in the United States and China. Even though AI systems are built, trained, and maintained through complex global labor chains, they reproduce existing inequalities. It is crucial to recognize the broader structures in which AI is embedded and carefully consider issues such as fairness, transparency, autonomy, and the protection of workers' changing roles and dignity. Finally, building collective *resilience* becomes essential not only for surviving but also for thriving during and after the ongoing change. Investing in supportive leadership, collaborative work environments, and learning opportunities can help workers adapt, maintain well-being, and continue contributing creatively to renewed AI-enabled workplaces.

This is the End

The new always happens against the overwhelming odds of statistical laws and their probability, which for all practical, everyday purposes amounts to certainty. Hannah Arendt (1998, p. 178) in *The Human Condition* (originally published 1958).

The future of AI has no predetermined path. The development of AI may sometimes feel like a journey upriver into territory that is only partially mapped, where the further we travel, the more uncertain the destination becomes. The AI transformation may feel unsettling as old assumptions about work, creativity, and human capability no longer fully apply. Perhaps this is the moment of self-realization at which humanity must face the existential question, who are we, and who do we choose to become? What keeps us willing to step off the edge and fall into uncertainty is our trust in people and in the future that is still unfolding. This is the human part of the story—about hope and meaning—and the belief that the paths ahead remain open.

Like many turning points in history, the future emerges from a series of decisions, conflicts, and compromises. The development of AI poses a major risk for societal sustainability, especially because of the potential rise of inequalities and the diminishing role of human work. However, humans have a role to play in the story. Human creativity is hard to replace, and AI can augment human creativity and provide new solutions and opportunities. Organizations have a responsibility to support and protect human creativity and meaningful work. Much will depend on how societies choose to govern and shape these technologies. If human-centered values prevail, the transformation of AI could begin a new phase of technological development in which AI expands the possibilities for meaningful human work.

References

Acemoglu, D. (2025a). The need for multipolar artificial intelligence governance. In L. Y. Ing & D. Rodrik (Eds.), *The new global economic order* (pp. 108–119). Routledge.

Acemoglu, D. (2025b). The simple macroeconomics of AI. *Economic Policy, 40*(121), 13–58. https://doi.org/10.1093/epolic/eiae042

Adel, A. (2022). Future of industry 5.0 in society: Human-centric solutions, challenges and prospective research areas. *Journal of Cloud Computing, 11*(1), 40. https://doi.org/10.1186/s13677-022-00314-5

Amabile, T. M., & Pratt, M. G. (2016). The dynamic componential model of creativity and innovation in organizations: Making progress, making meaning. *Research in Organizational Behavior, 36*, 157–183. https://doi.org/10.1016/j.riob.2016.10.001

Arendt, H. (1998). *The human condition* (2nd ed.). University of Chicago Press.

Bankins, S., & Formosa, P. (2023). The ethical implications of artificial intelligence (AI) for meaningful work. *Journal of Business Ethics, 185*(4), 725–740. https://doi.org/10.1007/s10551-023-05339-7

Baumeister, R. F. (2022). *The self explained: Why and how we become who we are.* Guilford Publications.

Borges, J. L. (1964). The garden of forking paths. In J. L. Borges (Ed.), *Labyrinths, selected stories and other writings* (pp. 19–29). New Directions Publishing Corporation.

Brynjolfsson, E., Chandar, B., & Chen, R. (2025a). Canaries in the coal mine? Six facts about the recent employment effects of artificial intelligence. Stanford Digital Economy Lab, Stanford University, https://digitaleconomy.stanford.edu/publications/canaries-in-the-coal-mine/

Brynjolfsson, E., Li, D., & Raymond, L. (2025b). Generative AI at work. *The Quarterly Journal of Economics, 140*(2), 889–942. https://doi.org/10.1093/qje/qjae044

Buttaboni, C., & Floridi, L. (2026). A regulatory taxonomy of AI opacity in the EU: rethinking transparency, traceability, interpretability, and explainability. *AI and Ethics, 6*(1), 100. https://doi.org/10.1007/s43681-025-00940-0

Cazzaniga, M., Pizzinelli, C., Rockall, E., & Tavares, M. M. (2025). Exposure to artificial intelligence and occupational mobility: A cross-country analysis. *Economía LACEA Journal, 24*(1), 314–339. https://doi.org/10.31389/eco.451

Cedefop. (2025). *Preparing for 2040: Four AI-powered scenarios for the future of continuing skills development.* Publications Office of the European Union. http://data.europa.eu/doi/10.2801/2114554

Cools, H., Van Gorp, B., & Opgenhaffen, M. (2024). Where exactly between utopia and dystopia? A framing analysis of AI and automation in US newspapers. *Journalism, 25*(1), 3–21. https://doi.org/10.1177/14648849221122647

Coxen, L., van der Vaart, L., Van den Broeck, A., & Rothmann, S. (2021). Basic psychological needs in the work context: A systematic literature review of diary studies. *Frontiers in Psychology, 12*, 698526. https://doi.org/10.3389/fpsyg.2021.698526

Czvetkó, T., Sebestyén, V., & Abonyi, J. (2025). Key factors of industry 5.0-based organizational sustainability. *Technology in Society, 83*, 102966. https://doi.org/10.1016/j.techsoc.2025.102966

Deci, E. L., & Ryan, R. M. (2000). The "what" and "why" of goal pursuits: Human needs and the self-determination of behavior. *Psychological Inquiry, 11*(4), 227–268. https://doi.org/10.1207/S15327965PLI1104_01

del Rio-Chanona, R. M., Ernst, E., Merola, R., Samaan, D., & Teutloff, O. (2025). AI and jobs. A review of theory, estimates, and evidence. ArXiv, Cornell University, https://doi.org/10.48550/arXiv.2509.15265

Emirbayer, M., & Mische, A. (1998). What is agency? *American Journal of Sociology, 103*(4), 962–1023. https://doi.org/10.1086/231294

Felin, T., & Holweg, M. (2024). Theory is all you need: AI, human cognition, and causal reasoning. *Strategy Science, 9*(4), 346–371. https://doi.org/10.1287/stsc.2024.0189

Floridi, L., Cowls, J., Beltrametti, M., Chatila, R., Chazerand, P., Dignum, V., Luetge, C., Madelin, R., Pagallo, U., Rossi, F., Schafer, B., Valcke, P., & Vayena, E. (2018). AI4People—An ethical framework for a good AI society: Opportunities, risks, principles, and recommendations. *Minds and Machines, 28*(4), 689–707. https://doi.org/10.1007/s11023-018-9482-5

Goller, D., Gschwendt, C., & Wolter, S. C. (2025). This time it's different–Generative artificial intelligence and occupational choice. *Labour Economics, 95*, 102746.

Gray, M. L., & Suri, S. (2019). *Ghost work: How to stop Silicon Valley from building a new global underclass.* Harper Business.

Haider, S. A., Borna, S., Gomez-Cabello, C. A., Pressman, S. M., Haider, C. R., & Forte, A. J. (2026). The algorithmic divide: A systematic review on AI-driven racial disparities in healthcare. *Journal of Racial and Ethnic Health Disparities, 13*(1), 188–217. https://doi.org/10.1007/s40615-024-02237-0

Heiskari, M., Celuch, M., Koivula, A., Savolainen, I., & Oksanen, A. (2025). Technological identity and basic psychological needs in the use of new technologies: A two-wave cross-national survey study. *International Journal of Information Management, 84*(October 2025), 102926. https://doi.org/10.1016/j.ijinfomgt.2025.102926

Heyden, M. L., Fourné, S. P., Koene, B. A., Werkman, R., & Ansari, S. (2017). Rethinking 'top-down' and 'bottom-up' roles of top and middle managers in organizational change: Implications for employee support. *Journal of Management Studies, 54*(7), 961–985. https://doi.org/10.1111/joms.12258

Kauhanen, A. & Rouvinen, P. (2026). *Artificial intelligence has not impacted youth labor market outcomes in Finland.* Memo 173. ETLA. https://www.etla.fi/julkaisut/muistiot/tekoaly-ei-ole-vaikuttanut-nuorten-tyomarkkina-asemaan-suomessa/

Latikka, R., Koivula, A., Bergdahl, J., & Oksanen, A. (2026). Digital relatedness: A longitudinal study on social resources and the use of smart technology. *New Media & Society, 28*(2), 652–672. https://doi.org/10.1177/14614448241295721

Li, L., & Duan, L. (2025). Human centric innovation at the heart of industry 5.0—Exploring research challenges and opportunities. *International Journal of Production Research, 63*(1), 1–33. https://doi.org/10.1080/00207543.2025.2462657

Mirbabaie, M., Brünker, F., Möllmann Frick, N. R., & Stieglitz, S. (2022). The rise of artificial intelligence–Understanding the AI identity threat at the workplace. *Electronic Markets, 32*(1), 73–99. https://doi.org/10.1007/s12525-021-00496-x

Muhammad, S. S., Dey, B. L., Kamal, M. M., Samuel, L., & Alzeiby, E. A. (2025). Digital transformation or digital divide? SMEs' use of AI during global crisis. *Technological Forecasting and Social Change, 217*, 124184. https://doi.org/10.1016/j.techfore.2025.124184

Muldoon, J., Cant, C., Wu, B., & Graham, M. (2024). A typology of artificial intelligence data work. *Big Data & Society, 11*(1), 1–13. https://doi.org/10.1177/20539517241232632

Noy, S., & Zhang, W. (2023). Experimental evidence on the productivity effects of generative artificial intelligence. *Science, 381*(6654), 187–192. https://doi.org/10.1126/science.adh2586

Oksanen, A., Osma, T., Heiskari, M., Cvetkovic, A., Soares Ruokosuo, E., Koike, M., Arriaga, P., & Savolainen, I. (2026). Mapping AI learning readiness self-efficacy worldwide: Scale validation and cross-continental patterns. *Computers in Human Behavior: Artificial Humans, 7*, 100251. https://doi.org/10.1016/j.chbah.2026.100251

Restrepo, P. (2025). *We won't be missed: Work and growth in the AGI world* (No. w34423). National Bureau of Economic Research.

Roth, E. (2026, February 26). *Burger King will use AI to check if employees say 'please' and 'thank you'*. The Verge. https://www.theverge.com/ai-artificial-intelligence/884911/burger-king-ai-assistant-patty

Sapkota, R., Roumeliotis, K. I., & Karkee, M. (2026). AI agents vs. agentic AI: A conceptual taxonomy, applications and challenges. *Information Fusion, 126*(Part B, February), 103599. https://doi.org/10.1016/j.inffus.2025.103599

Sarikaya, R. (2025). Path to artificial general intelligence: past, present, and future. *Annual Reviews in Control, 60*, 101021. https://doi.org/10.1016/j.arcontrol.2025.101021

Sarracino, F., & O'Connor, K. J. (2021). Economic growth and well-being beyond the Easterlin paradox. In *A modern guide to the economics of happiness* (pp. 162–188). Edward Elgar Publishing. https://doi.org/10.4337/9781788978767.00018

Savolainen, I., Ylinen, L., Grönroos, R., & Oksanen, A. (2026). AI transformation in working life: A systematic review of usage and attitudes towards AI among workers. *Digital Business, 6*(1), 100162. https://doi.org/10.1016/j.digbus.2025.100162

Stamboliev, E., & Christiaens, T. (2025). How empty is trustworthy AI? A discourse analysis of the ethics guidelines of trustworthy AI. *Critical Policy Studies, 19*(1), 39–56. https://doi.org/10.1080/19460171.2024.2315431

Stanford Institute for Human-Centered Artificial Intelligence (HAI). (2025). *Artificial Intelligence Index Report 2025*. Stanford University. https://hai.stanford.edu/ai-index/2025-ai-index-report

Suárez, D., & García-Mariñoso, B. (2025). On the verge of a digital divide in the use of generative AI? *Telecommunications Policy, 49*(7), 102997. https://doi.org/10.1016/j.telpol.2025.102997

Tubaro, P., Casilli, A. A., & Coville, M. (2020). The trainer, the verifier, the imitator: Three ways in which human platform workers support artificial intelligence. *Big Data & Society, 7*(1), 2053951720919776. https://doi.org/10.1177/2053951720919776

Van den Broeck, A., Ferris, D. L., Chang, C.-H., & Rosen, C. C. (2016). A review of self-determination theory's basic psychological needs at work. *Journal of Management, 42*(5), 1195–1229. https://doi.org/10.1177/0149206316632058

van Dijk, J. (2020). *The digital divide*. Polity.

World Economic Forum. (2025). *The future of jobs report 2025*. World Economic Forum. https://www.weforum.org/reports/the-future-of-jobs-report-2025

Yilmazkuday, H. (2025). Artificial intelligence and labor markets: evidence from Google Trends. *Journal of Economics and Finance, 49*(4), 1078–1093. https://doi.org/10.1007/s12197-025-09732-y

Appendix

This appendix lists the key measures used throughout the analyses presented in this book. For transparency and replicability, the items and scales are reported as used in the models, along with references to their original sources.

AILRSE-5

The Five-Item AI Learning Readiness Self-Efficacy (AILRSE-5, Oksanen et al., 2026). The items were developed by adapting earlier measures of technological self-efficacy (Igbaria & Iivari, 1995; Tsai et al., 2021; Turja et al., 2019).

	Item
1	I'm confident in my ability to understand how new AI technologies work.
2	I'm confident in my ability to learn how to use new AI technologies if necessary.
3	I'm confident in my ability to learn how to apply new AI technologies in my daily life.
4	I'm confident in my ability to learn how to use new AI technologies to solve a problem.
5	I'm confident in my ability to learn how to use new AI technologies independently.

A. Oksanen, I. Savolainen, *AI Disruption at Work*, Palgrave Advances in Work and Organizational Psychology,
https://doi.org/10.1007/978-3-032-35207-1

Note: Response options ranged from 1 (*strongly disagree*) to 7 (*strongly agree*). Higher scores indicate higher AI learning readiness self-efficacy.

AI Identity Threat

AI identity threat measures workers' perceived threat to their worth, competence, and authenticity. The measure was adapted from Craig et al. (2019) and Mirbabaie et al. (2022).

Worth Threat

	Item
1	AI makes me feel less respected by others in my peer group.
2	AI makes me feel others will consider me to be a poor member of my peer group.
3	AI makes me feel that people in my peer group will admire me less.
4	AI makes me feel that people in my peer group will lose respect for me.

Competence Threat

	Item
1	AI makes me feel less confident about having the skills needed to get work done.
2	AI makes me feel that I do things poorly.
3	AI makes me feel less confident that I understand things well enough to get work done.
4	AI makes me feel that I have less ability to get work done.

Authenticity Threat

	Item
1	AI makes me feel less like the person I want to be.
2	AI makes me feel discouraged with who I am.
3	AI makes me take a less positive attitude toward myself as a person.
4	AI makes me feel displeased with who I am.

Note: Response options ranged from 1 (*does not describe me at all*) to 7 (*describes me completely*). Higher scores indicate higher AI-induced identity threat.

Positive AI Attitude

We used a four-item version of the positivity dimension of the General Attitudes towards Artificial Intelligence Scale (GAAIS; Schepman & Rodway, 2020).

	Item
1	Artificial Intelligence can provide new economic opportunities for this country.
2	Artificial Intelligence can have positive impacts on people's wellbeing.
3	There are many beneficial applications of Artificial Intelligence.
4	Much of society will benefit from a future full of Artificial Intelligence.

Note: Response options ranged from 1 (*strongly disagree*) to 7 (*strongly agree*). Higher scores indicate more positive attitudes toward AI.

AI Stress

We examined AI stress using three items capturing AI-related strain. The items were adapted from measures used in previous research on technostress (Baabdullah, 2024; Westermann, 2017; Ragu-Nathan et al., 2008).

	Item
1	I am forced by AI to do more work than I can handle.
2	I am forced by AI to work with very tight time schedules.
3	I am forced to change my work habits to adapt to AI.

Note: Response options ranged from 1 (*strongly disagree*) to 7 (*strongly agree*). Higher scores indicate higher AI-related stress.

New Technology User Identity

In-group identification with new technology users was based on the 3-item centrality dimension of the of In-Group Identification Scale introduced by Leach et al. (2008).

	Item
1	I often think about the fact that I am a user of new technologies.
2	The fact that I am a user of new technologies is an important part of my identity.
3	Being a user of new technologies is an important part of how I see myself.

Note: Response options ranged from 1 (*strongly disagree*) to 7 (*strongly agree*). Higher scores indicate higher in-group identification with new technology users.

Index

A. Oksanen, I. Savolainen, *AI Disruption at Work*, Palgrave Advances in Work and Organizational Psychology,
https://doi.org/10.1007/978-3-032-35207-1

FSC
www.fsc.org
MIX
Papier | Fördert gute Waldnutzung
FSC® C083411

Kolibri 360 GmbH
Ferdinand-Jühlke-Straße 7
99095 Erfurt, Deutschland
produktsicherheit@kolibri360.de